C-585   CAREER EXAMINATION SERIES

This is your
PASSBOOK for...

Physical Therapist

Test Preparation Study Guide
Questions & Answers

NATIONAL LEARNING CORPORATION®

COPYRIGHT NOTICE

This book is SOLELY intended for, is sold ONLY to, and its use is RESTRICTED to individual, bona fide applicants or candidates who qualify by virtue of having seriously filed applications for appropriate license, certificate, professional and/or promotional advancement, higher school matriculation, scholarship, or other legitimate requirements of education and/or governmental authorities.

This book is NOT intended for use, class instruction, tutoring, training, duplication, copying, reprinting, excerption, or adaptation, etc., by:

1) Other publishers
2) Proprietors and/or Instructors of "Coaching" and/or Preparatory Courses
3) Personnel and/or Training Divisions of commercial, industrial, and governmental organizations
4) Schools, colleges, or universities and/or their departments and staffs, including teachers and other personnel
5) Testing Agencies or Bureaus
6) Study groups which seek by the purchase of a single volume to copy and/or duplicate and/or adapt this material for use by the group as a whole without having purchased individual volumes for each of the members of the group
7) Et al.

Such persons would be in violation of appropriate Federal and State statutes.

PROVISION OF LICENSING AGREEMENTS – Recognized educational, commercial, industrial, and governmental institutions and organizations, and others legitimately engaged in educational pursuits, including training, testing, and measurement activities, may address request for a licensing agreement to the copyright owners, who will determine whether, and under what conditions, including fees and charges, the materials in this book may be used them. In other words, a licensing facility exists for the legitimate use of the material in this book on other than an individual basis. However, it is asseverated and affirmed here that the material in this book CANNOT be used without the receipt of the express permission of such a licensing agreement from the Publishers. Inquiries re licensing should be addressed to the company, attention rights and permissions department.

All rights reserved, including the right of reproduction in whole or in part, in any form or by any means, electronic or mechanical, including photocopying, recording, or by any information storage and retrieval system, without permission in writing from the Publisher.

Copyright © 2024 by
National Learning Corporation

212 Michael Drive, Syosset, NY 11791
(516) 921-8888 • www.passbooks.com
E-mail: info@passbooks.com

PUBLISHED IN THE UNITED STATES OF AMERICA

PASSBOOK® SERIES

THE *PASSBOOK® SERIES* has been created to prepare applicants and candidates for the ultimate academic battlefield – the examination room.

At some time in our lives, each and every one of us may be required to take an examination – for validation, matriculation, admission, qualification, registration, certification, or licensure.

Based on the assumption that every applicant or candidate has met the basic formal educational standards, has taken the required number of courses, and read the necessary texts, the *PASSBOOK® SERIES* furnishes the one special preparation which may assure passing with confidence, instead of failing with insecurity. Examination questions – together with answers – are furnished as the basic vehicle for study so that the mysteries of the examination and its compounding difficulties may be eliminated or diminished by a sure method.

This book is meant to help you pass your examination provided that you qualify and are serious in your objective.

The entire field is reviewed through the huge store of content information which is succinctly presented through a provocative and challenging approach – the question-and-answer method.

A climate of success is established by furnishing the correct answers at the end of each test.

You soon learn to recognize types of questions, forms of questions, and patterns of questioning. You may even begin to anticipate expected outcomes.

You perceive that many questions are repeated or adapted so that you can gain acute insights, which may enable you to score many sure points.

You learn how to confront new questions, or types of questions, and to attack them confidently and work out the correct answers.

You note objectives and emphases, and recognize pitfalls and dangers, so that you may make positive educational adjustments.

Moreover, you are kept fully informed in relation to new concepts, methods, practices, and directions in the field.

You discover that you are actually taking the examination all the time: you are preparing for the examination by "taking" an examination, not by reading extraneous and/or supererogatory textbooks.

In short, this PASSBOOK®, used directedly, should be an important factor in helping you to pass your test.

PHYSICAL THERAPIST

DUTIES AND RESPONSIBILITIES
Under supervision, administers physical therapy in a hospital or clinic, or in other health programs for handicapped children. Employs physio-therapy and rehabilitation techniques in the treatment of home and clinic patients as prescribed and directed by a physician. Performs professional physical therapy evaluation and treatment; performs related duties as required.

EXAMPLES OF TYPICAL TASKS
Gives prescribed treatment in all branches of physical therapy, such as electrotherapy, hydrotherapy, actinotherapy, thermotherapy, massage, and therapeutic remedial exercise. Gives training in activities of daily living. Performs muscle, nerve, and other diagnostic tests, and records test results. Instructs and assists parents in the physical care and transportation of handicapped children. Interviews and screens applicants for care under the handicapped children program. Maintains and makes minor repairs to equipment. Orders supplies, keeps records, and makes reports.

SUBJECT OF EXAMINATION
The examination will be of the multiple-choice type and will be related to the duties of the position and related areas.

HOW TO TAKE A TEST

I. YOU MUST PASS AN EXAMINATION

A. *WHAT EVERY CANDIDATE SHOULD KNOW*

Examination applicants often ask us for help in preparing for the written test. What can I study in advance? What kinds of questions will be asked? How will the test be given? How will the papers be graded?

As an applicant for a civil service examination, you may be wondering about some of these things. Our purpose here is to suggest effective methods of advance study and to describe civil service examinations.

Your chances for success on this examination can be increased if you know how to prepare. Those "pre-examination jitters" can be reduced if you know what to expect. You can even experience an adventure in good citizenship if you know why civil service exams are given.

B. *WHY ARE CIVIL SERVICE EXAMINATIONS GIVEN?*

Civil service examinations are important to you in two ways. As a citizen, you want public jobs filled by employees who know how to do their work. As a job seeker, you want a fair chance to compete for that job on an equal footing with other candidates. The best-known means of accomplishing this two-fold goal is the competitive examination.

Exams are widely publicized throughout the nation. They may be administered for jobs in federal, state, city, municipal, town or village governments or agencies.

Any citizen may apply, with some limitations, such as the age or residence of applicants. Your experience and education may be reviewed to see whether you meet the requirements for the particular examination. When these requirements exist, they are reasonable and applied consistently to all applicants. Thus, a competitive examination may cause you some uneasiness now, but it is your privilege and safeguard.

C. *HOW ARE CIVIL SERVICE EXAMS DEVELOPED?*

Examinations are carefully written by trained technicians who are specialists in the field known as "psychological measurement," in consultation with recognized authorities in the field of work that the test will cover. These experts recommend the subject matter areas or skills to be tested; only those knowledges or skills important to your success on the job are included. The most reliable books and source materials available are used as references. Together, the experts and technicians judge the difficulty level of the questions.

Test technicians know how to phrase questions so that the problem is clearly stated. Their ethics do not permit "trick" or "catch" questions. Questions may have been tried out on sample groups, or subjected to statistical analysis, to determine their usefulness.

Written tests are often used in combination with performance tests, ratings of training and experience, and oral interviews. All of these measures combine to form the best-known means of finding the right person for the right job.

II. HOW TO PASS THE WRITTEN TEST

A. NATURE OF THE EXAMINATION

To prepare intelligently for civil service examinations, you should know how they differ from school examinations you have taken. In school you were assigned certain definite pages to read or subjects to cover. The examination questions were quite detailed and usually emphasized memory. Civil service exams, on the other hand, try to discover your present ability to perform the duties of a position, plus your potentiality to learn these duties. In other words, a civil service exam attempts to predict how successful you will be. Questions cover such a broad area that they cannot be as minute and detailed as school exam questions.

In the public service similar kinds of work, or positions, are grouped together in one "class." This process is known as *position-classification*. All the positions in a class are paid according to the salary range for that class. One class title covers all of these positions, and they are all tested by the same examination.

B. FOUR BASIC STEPS

1) Study the announcement

How, then, can you know what subjects to study? Our best answer is: "Learn as much as possible about the class of positions for which you've applied." The exam will test the knowledge, skills and abilities needed to do the work.

Your most valuable source of information about the position you want is the official exam announcement. This announcement lists the training and experience qualifications. Check these standards and apply only if you come reasonably close to meeting them.

The brief description of the position in the examination announcement offers some clues to the subjects which will be tested. Think about the job itself. Review the duties in your mind. Can you perform them, or are there some in which you are rusty? Fill in the blank spots in your preparation.

Many jurisdictions preview the written test in the exam announcement by including a section called "Knowledge and Abilities Required," "Scope of the Examination," or some similar heading. Here you will find out specifically what fields will be tested.

2) Review your own background

Once you learn in general what the position is all about, and what you need to know to do the work, ask yourself which subjects you already know fairly well and which need improvement. You may wonder whether to concentrate on improving your strong areas or on building some background in your fields of weakness. When the announcement has specified "some knowledge" or "considerable knowledge," or has used adjectives like "beginning principles of…" or "advanced … methods," you can get a clue as to the number and difficulty of questions to be asked in any given field. More questions, and hence broader coverage, would be included for those subjects which are more important in the work. Now weigh your strengths and weaknesses against the job requirements and prepare accordingly.

3) Determine the level of the position

Another way to tell how intensively you should prepare is to understand the level of the job for which you are applying. Is it the entering level? In other words, is this the position in which beginners in a field of work are hired? Or is it an intermediate or advanced level? Sometimes this is indicated by such words as "Junior" or "Senior" in the class title. Other jurisdictions use Roman numerals to designate the level – Clerk I, Clerk II, for example. The word "Supervisor" sometimes appears in the title. If the level is not indicated by the title, check the description of duties. Will you be working under very close supervision, or will you have responsibility for independent decisions in this work?

4) Choose appropriate study materials

Now that you know the subjects to be examined and the relative amount of each subject to be covered, you can choose suitable study materials. For beginning level jobs, or even advanced ones, if you have a pronounced weakness in some aspect of your training, read a modern, standard textbook in that field. Be sure it is up to date and has general coverage. Such books are normally available at your library, and the librarian will be glad to help you locate one. For entry-level positions, questions of appropriate difficulty are chosen – neither highly advanced questions, nor those too simple. Such questions require careful thought but not advanced training.

If the position for which you are applying is technical or advanced, you will read more advanced, specialized material. If you are already familiar with the basic principles of your field, elementary textbooks would waste your time. Concentrate on advanced textbooks and technical periodicals. Think through the concepts and review difficult problems in your field.

These are all general sources. You can get more ideas on your own initiative, following these leads. For example, training manuals and publications of the government agency which employs workers in your field can be useful, particularly for technical and professional positions. A letter or visit to the government department involved may result in more specific study suggestions, and certainly will provide you with a more definite idea of the exact nature of the position you are seeking.

III. KINDS OF TESTS

Tests are used for purposes other than measuring knowledge and ability to perform specified duties. For some positions, it is equally important to test ability to make adjustments to new situations or to profit from training. In others, basic mental abilities not dependent on information are essential. Questions which test these things may not appear as pertinent to the duties of the position as those which test for knowledge and information. Yet they are often highly important parts of a fair examination. For very general questions, it is almost impossible to help you direct your study efforts. What we can do is to point out some of the more common of these general abilities needed in public service positions and describe some typical questions.

1) General information

Broad, general information has been found useful for predicting job success in some kinds of work. This is tested in a variety of ways, from vocabulary lists to questions about current events. Basic background in some field of work, such as sociology or economics, may be sampled in a group of questions. Often these are principles which have become familiar to most persons through exposure rather than through formal training. It is difficult to advise you how to study for these questions; being alert to the world around you is our best suggestion.

2) Verbal ability

An example of an ability needed in many positions is verbal or language ability. Verbal ability is, in brief, the ability to use and understand words. Vocabulary and grammar tests are typical measures of this ability. Reading comprehension or paragraph interpretation questions are common in many kinds of civil service tests. You are given a paragraph of written material and asked to find its central meaning.

3) Numerical ability

Number skills can be tested by the familiar arithmetic problem, by checking paired lists of numbers to see which are alike and which are different, or by interpreting charts and graphs. In the latter test, a graph may be printed in the test booklet which you are asked to use as the basis for answering questions.

4) Observation

A popular test for law-enforcement positions is the observation test. A picture is shown to you for several minutes, then taken away. Questions about the picture test your ability to observe both details and larger elements.

5) Following directions

In many positions in the public service, the employee must be able to carry out written instructions dependably and accurately. You may be given a chart with several columns, each column listing a variety of information. The questions require you to carry out directions involving the information given in the chart.

6) Skills and aptitudes

Performance tests effectively measure some manual skills and aptitudes. When the skill is one in which you are trained, such as typing or shorthand, you can practice. These tests are often very much like those given in business school or high school courses. For many of the other skills and aptitudes, however, no short-time preparation can be made. Skills and abilities natural to you or that you have developed throughout your lifetime are being tested.

Many of the general questions just described provide all the data needed to answer the questions and ask you to use your reasoning ability to find the answers. Your best preparation for these tests, as well as for tests of facts and ideas, is to be at your physical and mental best. You, no doubt, have your own methods of getting into an exam-taking mood and keeping "in shape." The next section lists some ideas on this subject.

IV. KINDS OF QUESTIONS

Only rarely is the "essay" question, which you answer in narrative form, used in civil service tests. Civil service tests are usually of the short-answer type. Full instructions for answering these questions will be given to you at the examination. But in case this is your first experience with short-answer questions and separate answer sheets, here is what you need to know:

1) Multiple-choice Questions

Most popular of the short-answer questions is the "multiple choice" or "best answer" question. It can be used, for example, to test for factual knowledge, ability to solve problems or judgment in meeting situations found at work.

A multiple-choice question is normally one of three types—
- It can begin with an incomplete statement followed by several possible endings. You are to find the one ending which *best* completes the statement, although some of the others may not be entirely wrong.
- It can also be a complete statement in the form of a question which is answered by choosing one of the statements listed.

- It can be in the form of a problem – again you select the best answer.

Here is an example of a multiple-choice question with a discussion which should give you some clues as to the method for choosing the right answer:

When an employee has a complaint about his assignment, the action which will *best* help him overcome his difficulty is to
- A. discuss his difficulty with his coworkers
- B. take the problem to the head of the organization
- C. take the problem to the person who gave him the assignment
- D. say nothing to anyone about his complaint

In answering this question, you should study each of the choices to find which is best. Consider choice "A" – Certainly an employee may discuss his complaint with fellow employees, but no change or improvement can result, and the complaint remains unresolved. Choice "B" is a poor choice since the head of the organization probably does not know what assignment you have been given, and taking your problem to him is known as "going over the head" of the supervisor. The supervisor, or person who made the assignment, is the person who can clarify it or correct any injustice. Choice "C" is, therefore, correct. To say nothing, as in choice "D," is unwise. Supervisors have and interest in knowing the problems employees are facing, and the employee is seeking a solution to his problem.

2) True/False Questions

The "true/false" or "right/wrong" form of question is sometimes used. Here a complete statement is given. Your job is to decide whether the statement is right or wrong.

SAMPLE: A roaming cell-phone call to a nearby city costs less than a non-roaming call to a distant city.

This statement is wrong, or false, since roaming calls are more expensive.

This is not a complete list of all possible question forms, although most of the others are variations of these common types. You will always get complete directions for answering questions. Be sure you understand *how* to mark your answers – ask questions until you do.

V. RECORDING YOUR ANSWERS

Computer terminals are used more and more today for many different kinds of exams.

For an examination with very few applicants, you may be told to record your answers in the test booklet itself. Separate answer sheets are much more common. If this separate answer sheet is to be scored by machine – and this is often the case – it is highly important that you mark your answers correctly in order to get credit.

An electronic scoring machine is often used in civil service offices because of the speed with which papers can be scored. Machine-scored answer sheets must be marked with a pencil, which will be given to you. This pencil has a high graphite content which responds to the electronic scoring machine. As a matter of fact, stray dots may register as answers, so do not let your pencil rest on the answer sheet while you are pondering the correct answer. Also, if your pencil lead breaks or is otherwise defective, ask for another.

Since the answer sheet will be dropped in a slot in the scoring machine, be careful not to bend the corners or get the paper crumpled.

The answer sheet normally has five vertical columns of numbers, with 30 numbers to a column. These numbers correspond to the question numbers in your test booklet. After each number, going across the page are four or five pairs of dotted lines. These short dotted lines have small letters or numbers above them. The first two pairs may also have a "T" or "F" above the letters. This indicates that the first two pairs only are to be used if the questions are of the true-false type. If the questions are multiple choice, disregard the "T" and "F" and pay attention only to the small letters or numbers.

Answer your questions in the manner of the sample that follows:

32. The largest city in the United States is
    A. Washington, D.C.
    B. New York City
    C. Chicago
    D. Detroit
    E. San Francisco

1) Choose the answer you think is best. (New York City is the largest, so "B" is correct.)
2) Find the row of dotted lines numbered the same as the question you are answering. (Find row number 32)
3) Find the pair of dotted lines corresponding to the answer. (Find the pair of lines under the mark "B.")
4) Make a solid black mark between the dotted lines.

VI. BEFORE THE TEST

Common sense will help you find procedures to follow to get ready for an examination. Too many of us, however, overlook these sensible measures. Indeed, nervousness and fatigue have been found to be the most serious reasons why applicants fail to do their best on civil service tests. Here is a list of reminders:

- Begin your preparation early – Don't wait until the last minute to go scurrying around for books and materials or to find out what the position is all about.
- Prepare continuously – An hour a night for a week is better than an all-night cram session. This has been definitely established. What is more, a night a week for a month will return better dividends than crowding your study into a shorter period of time.
- Locate the place of the exam – You have been sent a notice telling you when and where to report for the examination. If the location is in a different town or otherwise unfamiliar to you, it would be well to inquire the best route and learn something about the building.
- Relax the night before the test – Allow your mind to rest. Do not study at all that night. Plan some mild recreation or diversion; then go to bed early and get a good night's sleep.
- Get up early enough to make a leisurely trip to the place for the test – This way unforeseen events, traffic snarls, unfamiliar buildings, etc. will not upset you.
- Dress comfortably – A written test is not a fashion show. You will be known by number and not by name, so wear something comfortable.

- Leave excess paraphernalia at home – Shopping bags and odd bundles will get in your way. You need bring only the items mentioned in the official notice you received; usually everything you need is provided. Do not bring reference books to the exam. They will only confuse those last minutes and be taken away from you when in the test room.
- Arrive somewhat ahead of time – If because of transportation schedules you must get there very early, bring a newspaper or magazine to take your mind off yourself while waiting.
- Locate the examination room – When you have found the proper room, you will be directed to the seat or part of the room where you will sit. Sometimes you are given a sheet of instructions to read while you are waiting. Do not fill out any forms until you are told to do so; just read them and be prepared.
- Relax and prepare to listen to the instructions
- If you have any physical problem that may keep you from doing your best, be sure to tell the test administrator. If you are sick or in poor health, you really cannot do your best on the exam. You can come back and take the test some other time.

VII. AT THE TEST

The day of the test is here and you have the test booklet in your hand. The temptation to get going is very strong. Caution! There is more to success than knowing the right answers. You must know how to identify your papers and understand variations in the type of short-answer question used in this particular examination. Follow these suggestions for maximum results from your efforts:

1) Cooperate with the monitor

The test administrator has a duty to create a situation in which you can be as much at ease as possible. He will give instructions, tell you when to begin, check to see that you are marking your answer sheet correctly, and so on. He is not there to guard you, although he will see that your competitors do not take unfair advantage. He wants to help you do your best.

2) Listen to all instructions

Don't jump the gun! Wait until you understand all directions. In most civil service tests you get more time than you need to answer the questions. So don't be in a hurry. Read each word of instructions until you clearly understand the meaning. Study the examples, listen to all announcements and follow directions. Ask questions if you do not understand what to do.

3) Identify your papers

Civil service exams are usually identified by number only. You will be assigned a number; you must not put your name on your test papers. Be sure to copy your number correctly. Since more than one exam may be given, copy your exact examination title.

4) Plan your time

Unless you are told that a test is a "speed" or "rate of work" test, speed itself is usually not important. Time enough to answer all the questions will be provided, but this does not mean that you have all day. An overall time limit has been set. Divide the total time (in minutes) by the number of questions to determine the approximate time you have for each question.

5) Do not linger over difficult questions

If you come across a difficult question, mark it with a paper clip (useful to have along) and come back to it when you have been through the booklet. One caution if you do this – be sure to skip a number on your answer sheet as well. Check often to be sure that you have not lost your place and that you are marking in the row numbered the same as the question you are answering.

6) Read the questions

Be sure you know what the question asks! Many capable people are unsuccessful because they failed to *read* the questions correctly.

7) Answer all questions

Unless you have been instructed that a penalty will be deducted for incorrect answers, it is better to guess than to omit a question.

8) Speed tests

It is often better NOT to guess on speed tests. It has been found that on timed tests people are tempted to spend the last few seconds before time is called in marking answers at random – without even reading them – in the hope of picking up a few extra points. To discourage this practice, the instructions may warn you that your score will be "corrected" for guessing. That is, a penalty will be applied. The incorrect answers will be deducted from the correct ones, or some other penalty formula will be used.

9) Review your answers

If you finish before time is called, go back to the questions you guessed or omitted to give them further thought. Review other answers if you have time.

10) Return your test materials

If you are ready to leave before others have finished or time is called, take ALL your materials to the monitor and leave quietly. Never take any test material with you. The monitor can discover whose papers are not complete, and taking a test booklet may be grounds for disqualification.

VIII. EXAMINATION TECHNIQUES

1) Read the general instructions carefully. These are usually printed on the first page of the exam booklet. As a rule, these instructions refer to the timing of the examination; the fact that you should not start work until the signal and must stop work at a signal, etc. If there are any *special* instructions, such as a choice of questions to be answered, make sure that you note this instruction carefully.

2) When you are ready to start work on the examination, that is as soon as the signal has been given, read the instructions to each question booklet, underline any key words or phrases, such as *least, best, outline, describe* and the like. In this way you will tend to answer as requested rather than discover on reviewing your paper that you *listed without describing*, that you selected the *worst* choice rather than the *best* choice, etc.

3) If the examination is of the objective or multiple-choice type – that is, each question will also give a series of possible answers: A, B, C or D, and you are called upon to select the best answer and write the letter next to that answer on your answer paper – it is advisable to start answering each question in turn. There may be anywhere from 50 to 100 such questions in the three or four hours allotted and you can see how much time would be taken if you read through all the questions before beginning to answer any. Furthermore, if you come across a question or group of questions which you know would be difficult to answer, it would undoubtedly affect your handling of all the other questions.

4) If the examination is of the essay type and contains but a few questions, it is a moot point as to whether you should read all the questions before starting to answer any one. Of course, if you are given a choice – say five out of seven and the like – then it is essential to read all the questions so you can eliminate the two that are most difficult. If, however, you are asked to answer all the questions, there may be danger in trying to answer the easiest one first because you may find that you will spend too much time on it. The best technique is to answer the first question, then proceed to the second, etc.

5) Time your answers. Before the exam begins, write down the time it started, then add the time allowed for the examination and write down the time it must be completed, then divide the time available somewhat as follows:
   - If 3-1/2 hours are allowed, that would be 210 minutes. If you have 80 objective-type questions, that would be an average of 2-1/2 minutes per question. Allow yourself no more than 2 minutes per question, or a total of 160 minutes, which will permit about 50 minutes to review.
   - If for the time allotment of 210 minutes there are 7 essay questions to answer, that would average about 30 minutes a question. Give yourself only 25 minutes per question so that you have about 35 minutes to review.

6) The most important instruction is to *read each question* and make sure you know what is wanted. The second most important instruction is to *time yourself properly* so that you answer every question. The third most important instruction is to *answer every question*. Guess if you have to but include something for each question. Remember that you will receive no credit for a blank and will probably receive some credit if you write something in answer to an essay question. If you guess a letter – say "B" for a multiple-choice question – you may have guessed right. If you leave a blank as an answer to a multiple-choice question, the examiners may respect your feelings but it will not add a point to your score. Some exams may penalize you for wrong answers, so in such cases *only*, you may not want to guess unless you have some basis for your answer.

7) Suggestions
   a. Objective-type questions
      1. Examine the question booklet for proper sequence of pages and questions
      2. Read all instructions carefully
      3. Skip any question which seems too difficult; return to it after all other questions have been answered
      4. Apportion your time properly; do not spend too much time on any single question or group of questions

5. Note and underline key words – *all, most, fewest, least, best, worst, same, opposite,* etc.
6. Pay particular attention to negatives
7. Note unusual option, e.g., unduly long, short, complex, different or similar in content to the body of the question
8. Observe the use of "hedging" words – *probably, may, most likely,* etc.
9. Make sure that your answer is put next to the same number as the question
10. Do not second-guess unless you have good reason to believe the second answer is definitely more correct
11. Cross out original answer if you decide another answer is more accurate; do not erase until you are ready to hand your paper in
12. Answer all questions; guess unless instructed otherwise
13. Leave time for review

  b. Essay questions
    1. Read each question carefully
    2. Determine exactly what is wanted. Underline key words or phrases.
    3. Decide on outline or paragraph answer
    4. Include many different points and elements unless asked to develop any one or two points or elements
    5. Show impartiality by giving pros and cons unless directed to select one side only
    6. Make and write down any assumptions you find necessary to answer the questions
    7. Watch your English, grammar, punctuation and choice of words
    8. Time your answers; don't crowd material

8) Answering the essay question

Most essay questions can be answered by framing the specific response around several key words or ideas. Here are a few such key words or ideas:

M's: manpower, materials, methods, money, management
P's: purpose, program, policy, plan, procedure, practice, problems, pitfalls, personnel, public relations
  a. Six basic steps in handling problems:
    1. Preliminary plan and background development
    2. Collect information, data and facts
    3. Analyze and interpret information, data and facts
    4. Analyze and develop solutions as well as make recommendations
    5. Prepare report and sell recommendations
    6. Install recommendations and follow up effectiveness

  b. Pitfalls to avoid
    1. *Taking things for granted* – A statement of the situation does not necessarily imply that each of the elements is necessarily true; for example, a complaint may be invalid and biased so that all that can be taken for granted is that a complaint has been registered

2. *Considering only one side of a situation* – Wherever possible, indicate several alternatives and then point out the reasons you selected the best one
3. *Failing to indicate follow up* – Whenever your answer indicates action on your part, make certain that you will take proper follow-up action to see how successful your recommendations, procedures or actions turn out to be
4. *Taking too long in answering any single question* – Remember to time your answers properly

IX. AFTER THE TEST

Scoring procedures differ in detail among civil service jurisdictions although the general principles are the same. Whether the papers are hand-scored or graded by machine we have described, they are nearly always graded by number. That is, the person who marks the paper knows only the number – never the name – of the applicant. Not until all the papers have been graded will they be matched with names. If other tests, such as training and experience or oral interview ratings have been given, scores will be combined. Different parts of the examination usually have different weights. For example, the written test might count 60 percent of the final grade, and a rating of training and experience 40 percent. In many jurisdictions, veterans will have a certain number of points added to their grades.

After the final grade has been determined, the names are placed in grade order and an eligible list is established. There are various methods for resolving ties between those who get the same final grade – probably the most common is to place first the name of the person whose application was received first. Job offers are made from the eligible list in the order the names appear on it. You will be notified of your grade and your rank as soon as all these computations have been made. This will be done as rapidly as possible.

People who are found to meet the requirements in the announcement are called "eligibles." Their names are put on a list of eligible candidates. An eligible's chances of getting a job depend on how high he stands on this list and how fast agencies are filling jobs from the list.

When a job is to be filled from a list of eligibles, the agency asks for the names of people on the list of eligibles for that job. When the civil service commission receives this request, it sends to the agency the names of the three people highest on this list. Or, if the job to be filled has specialized requirements, the office sends the agency the names of the top three persons who meet these requirements from the general list.

The appointing officer makes a choice from among the three people whose names were sent to him. If the selected person accepts the appointment, the names of the others are put back on the list to be considered for future openings.

That is the rule in hiring from all kinds of eligible lists, whether they are for typist, carpenter, chemist, or something else. For every vacancy, the appointing officer has his choice of any one of the top three eligibles on the list. This explains why the person whose name is on top of the list sometimes does not get an appointment when some of the persons lower on the list do. If the appointing officer chooses the second or third eligible, the No. 1 eligible does not get a job at once, but stays on the list until he is appointed or the list is terminated.

X. HOW TO PASS THE INTERVIEW TEST

The examination for which you applied requires an oral interview test. You have already taken the written test and you are now being called for the interview test – the final part of the formal examination.

You may think that it is not possible to prepare for an interview test and that there are no procedures to follow during an interview. Our purpose is to point out some things you can do in advance that will help you and some good rules to follow and pitfalls to avoid while you are being interviewed.

What is an interview supposed to test?

The written examination is designed to test the technical knowledge and competence of the candidate; the oral is designed to evaluate intangible qualities, not readily measured otherwise, and to establish a list showing the relative fitness of each candidate – as measured against his competitors – for the position sought. Scoring is not on the basis of "right" and "wrong," but on a sliding scale of values ranging from "not passable" to "outstanding." As a matter of fact, it is possible to achieve a relatively low score without a single "incorrect" answer because of evident weakness in the qualities being measured.

Occasionally, an examination may consist entirely of an oral test – either an individual or a group oral. In such cases, information is sought concerning the technical knowledges and abilities of the candidate, since there has been no written examination for this purpose. More commonly, however, an oral test is used to supplement a written examination.

Who conducts interviews?

The composition of oral boards varies among different jurisdictions. In nearly all, a representative of the personnel department serves as chairman. One of the members of the board may be a representative of the department in which the candidate would work. In some cases, "outside experts" are used, and, frequently, a businessman or some other representative of the general public is asked to serve. Labor and management or other special groups may be represented. The aim is to secure the services of experts in the appropriate field.

However the board is composed, it is a good idea (and not at all improper or unethical) to ascertain in advance of the interview who the members are and what groups they represent. When you are introduced to them, you will have some idea of their backgrounds and interests, and at least you will not stutter and stammer over their names.

What should be done before the interview?

While knowledge about the board members is useful and takes some of the surprise element out of the interview, there is other preparation which is more substantive. It *is* possible to prepare for an oral interview – in several ways:

1) Keep a copy of your application and review it carefully before the interview

This may be the only document before the oral board, and the starting point of the interview. Know what education and experience you have listed there, and the sequence and dates of all of it. Sometimes the board will ask you to review the highlights of your experience for them; you should not have to hem and haw doing it.

2) Study the class specification and the examination announcement

Usually, the oral board has one or both of these to guide them. The qualities, characteristics or knowledges required by the position sought are stated in these documents. They offer valuable clues as to the nature of the oral interview. For example, if the job involves supervisory responsibilities, the announcement will usually indicate that knowledge of modern supervisory methods and the qualifications of the candidate as a supervisor will be tested. If so, you can expect such questions, frequently in the form of a hypothetical situation which you are expected to solve. NEVER go into an oral without knowledge of the duties and responsibilities of the job you seek.

3) Think through each qualification required

Try to visualize the kind of questions you would ask if you were a board member. How well could you answer them? Try especially to appraise your own knowledge and background in each area, *measured against the job sought*, and identify any areas in which you are weak. Be critical and realistic – do not flatter yourself.

4) Do some general reading in areas in which you feel you may be weak

For example, if the job involves supervision and your past experience has NOT, some general reading in supervisory methods and practices, particularly in the field of human relations, might be useful. Do NOT study agency procedures or detailed manuals. The oral board will be testing your understanding and capacity, not your memory.

5) Get a good night's sleep and watch your general health and mental attitude

You will want a clear head at the interview. Take care of a cold or any other minor ailment, and of course, no hangovers.

What should be done on the day of the interview?

Now comes the day of the interview itself. Give yourself plenty of time to get there. Plan to arrive somewhat ahead of the scheduled time, particularly if your appointment is in the fore part of the day. If a previous candidate fails to appear, the board might be ready for you a bit early. By early afternoon an oral board is almost invariably behind schedule if there are many candidates, and you may have to wait. Take along a book or magazine to read, or your application to review, but leave any extraneous material in the waiting room when you go in for your interview. In any event, relax and compose yourself.

The matter of dress is important. The board is forming impressions about you – from your experience, your manners, your attitude, and your appearance. Give your personal appearance careful attention. Dress your best, but not your flashiest. Choose conservative, appropriate clothing, and be sure it is immaculate. This is a business interview, and your appearance should indicate that you regard it as such. Besides, being well groomed and properly dressed will help boost your confidence.

Sooner or later, someone will call your name and escort you into the interview room. *This is it.* From here on you are on your own. It is too late for any more preparation. But remember, you asked for this opportunity to prove your fitness, and you are here because your request was granted.

What happens when you go in?

The usual sequence of events will be as follows: The clerk (who is often the board stenographer) will introduce you to the chairman of the oral board, who will introduce you to the other members of the board. Acknowledge the introductions before you sit down. Do not be surprised if you find a microphone facing you or a stenotypist sitting by. Oral interviews are usually recorded in the event of an appeal or other review.

Usually the chairman of the board will open the interview by reviewing the highlights of your education and work experience from your application – primarily for the benefit of the other members of the board, as well as to get the material into the record. Do not interrupt or comment unless there is an error or significant misinterpretation; if that is the case, do not hesitate. But do not quibble about insignificant matters. Also, he will usually ask you some question about your education, experience or your present job – partly to get you to start talking and to establish the interviewing "rapport." He may start the actual questioning, or turn it over to one of the other members. Frequently, each member undertakes the questioning on a particular area, one in which he is perhaps most competent, so you can expect each member to participate in the examination. Because time is limited, you may also expect some rather abrupt switches in the direction the questioning takes, so do not be upset by it. Normally, a board member will not pursue a single line of questioning unless he discovers a particular strength or weakness.

After each member has participated, the chairman will usually ask whether any member has any further questions, then will ask you if you have anything you wish to add. Unless you are expecting this question, it may floor you. Worse, it may start you off on an extended, extemporaneous speech. The board is not usually seeking more information. The question is principally to offer you a last opportunity to present further qualifications or to indicate that you have nothing to add. So, if you feel that a significant qualification or characteristic has been overlooked, it is proper to point it out in a sentence or so. Do not compliment the board on the thoroughness of their examination – they have been sketchy, and you know it. If you wish, merely say, "No thank you, I have nothing further to add." This is a point where you can "talk yourself out" of a good impression or fail to present an important bit of information. Remember, *you close the interview yourself*.

The chairman will then say, "That is all, Mr. _____, thank you." Do not be startled; the interview is over, and quicker than you think. Thank him, gather your belongings and take your leave. Save your sigh of relief for the other side of the door.

How to put your best foot forward

Throughout this entire process, you may feel that the board individually and collectively is trying to pierce your defenses, seek out your hidden weaknesses and embarrass and confuse you. Actually, this is not true. They are obliged to make an appraisal of your qualifications for the job you are seeking, and they want to see you in your best light. Remember, they must interview all candidates and a non-cooperative candidate may become a failure in spite of their best efforts to bring out his qualifications. Here are 15 suggestions that will help you:

1) **Be natural – Keep your attitude confident, not cocky**

If you are not confident that you can do the job, do not expect the board to be. Do not apologize for your weaknesses, try to bring out your strong points. The board is interested in a positive, not negative, presentation. Cockiness will antagonize any board member and make him wonder if you are covering up a weakness by a false show of strength.

2) **Get comfortable, but don't lounge or sprawl**

Sit erectly but not stiffly. A careless posture may lead the board to conclude that you are careless in other things, or at least that you are not impressed by the importance of the occasion. Either conclusion is natural, even if incorrect. Do not fuss with your clothing, a pencil or an ashtray. Your hands may occasionally be useful to emphasize a point; do not let them become a point of distraction.

3) **Do not wisecrack or make small talk**

This is a serious situation, and your attitude should show that you consider it as such. Further, the time of the board is limited – they do not want to waste it, and neither should you.

4) Do not exaggerate your experience or abilities
In the first place, from information in the application or other interviews and sources, the board may know more about you than you think. Secondly, you probably will not get away with it. An experienced board is rather adept at spotting such a situation, so do not take the chance.

5) If you know a board member, do not make a point of it, yet do not hide it
Certainly you are not fooling him, and probably not the other members of the board. Do not try to take advantage of your acquaintanceship – it will probably do you little good.

6) Do not dominate the interview
Let the board do that. They will give you the clues – do not assume that you have to do all the talking. Realize that the board has a number of questions to ask you, and do not try to take up all the interview time by showing off your extensive knowledge of the answer to the first one.

7) Be attentive
You only have 20 minutes or so, and you should keep your attention at its sharpest throughout. When a member is addressing a problem or question to you, give him your undivided attention. Address your reply principally to him, but do not exclude the other board members.

8) Do not interrupt
A board member may be stating a problem for you to analyze. He will ask you a question when the time comes. Let him state the problem, and wait for the question.

9) Make sure you understand the question
Do not try to answer until you are sure what the question is. If it is not clear, restate it in your own words or ask the board member to clarify it for you. However, do not haggle about minor elements.

10) Reply promptly but not hastily
A common entry on oral board rating sheets is "candidate responded readily," or "candidate hesitated in replies." Respond as promptly and quickly as you can, but do not jump to a hasty, ill-considered answer.

11) Do not be peremptory in your answers
A brief answer is proper – but do not fire your answer back. That is a losing game from your point of view. The board member can probably ask questions much faster than you can answer them.

12) Do not try to create the answer you think the board member wants
He is interested in what kind of mind you have and how it works – not in playing games. Furthermore, he can usually spot this practice and will actually grade you down on it.

13) Do not switch sides in your reply merely to agree with a board member
Frequently, a member will take a contrary position merely to draw you out and to see if you are willing and able to defend your point of view. Do not start a debate, yet do not surrender a good position. If a position is worth taking, it is worth defending.

14) Do not be afraid to admit an error in judgment if you are shown to be wrong

The board knows that you are forced to reply without any opportunity for careful consideration. Your answer may be demonstrably wrong. If so, admit it and get on with the interview.

15) Do not dwell at length on your present job

The opening question may relate to your present assignment. Answer the question but do not go into an extended discussion. You are being examined for a *new* job, not your present one. As a matter of fact, try to phrase ALL your answers in terms of the job for which you are being examined.

Basis of Rating

Probably you will forget most of these "do's" and "don'ts" when you walk into the oral interview room. Even remembering them all will not ensure you a passing grade. Perhaps you did not have the qualifications in the first place. But remembering them will help you to put your best foot forward, without treading on the toes of the board members.

Rumor and popular opinion to the contrary notwithstanding, an oral board wants you to make the best appearance possible. They know you are under pressure – but they also want to see how you respond to it as a guide to what your reaction would be under the pressures of the job you seek. They will be influenced by the degree of poise you display, the personal traits you show and the manner in which you respond.

ABOUT THIS BOOK

This book contains tests divided into Examination Sections. Go through each test, answering every question in the margin. We have also attached a sample answer sheet at the back of the book that can be removed and used. At the end of each test look at the answer key and check your answers. On the ones you got wrong, look at the right answer choice and learn. Do not fill in the answers first. Do not memorize the questions and answers, but understand the answer and principles involved. On your test, the questions will likely be different from the samples. Questions are changed and new ones added. If you understand these past questions you should have success with any changes that arise. Tests may consist of several types of questions. We have additional books on each subject should more study be advisable or necessary for you. Finally, the more you study, the better prepared you will be. This book is intended to be the last thing you study before you walk into the examination room. Prior study of relevant texts is also recommended. NLC publishes some of these in our Fundamental Series. Knowledge and good sense are important factors in passing your exam. Good luck also helps. So now study this Passbook, absorb the material contained within and take that knowledge into the examination. Then do your best to pass that exam.

EXAMINATION SECTION

ANATOMY & KINESIOLOGY

EXAMINATION SECTION
TEST 1

DIRECTIONS: Each question or incomplete statement is followed by several suggested answers or completions. Select the one that BEST answers the question or completes the statement. *PRINT THE LETTER OF THE COERECT ANSWER IN THE SPACE AT THE RIGHT.*

1. Which of the following anatomical reference terms refers to the midline of the body toward the attached end of the limb? 1.____
   A. Medial   B. Lateral   C. Proximal   D. Distal

2. The imaginary longitudinal line that divides the body into right and left parts is called the _____ plane. 2.____
   A. sagittal   B. frontal
   C. transverse   D. dorsal

3. Microscopic blood vessels where the exchange of nutrients and metabolic waste products take place are called 3.____
   A. venuoles   B. arterioles
   C. capillaries   D. none of the above

4. If torn or stressed beyond its ability to recoil, this connective tissue remains loose and nonfunctional until repaired by a physician. 4.____
   A. Tendon   B. Ligament
   C. Cartilage   D. Synovial capsule

5. Which of the following are movements in the frontal plane? 5.____
   A. Abduction, adduction   B. Elevation, depression
   C. Lateral flexion   D. All of the above

6. Most muscles are arranged in opposing pairs. When one muscle is contracting to achieve a desired movement (agonist), its opposite muscle (antagonist) is being stretched.
The antagonist to the muscles biceps femoris, semitendinosus, and semimembranosus is 6.____
   A. rectus femoris   B. psoas
   C. gluteus maximus   D. none of the above

7. Flexion of the knee joint is caused by 7.____
   A. sartorius   B. vastus medialis
   C. gastroenemius   D. all of the above

8. Twisting bent-knee situps will effectively strengthen the 8.____
   A. rectus abdominis
   B. transverse abdominis

1

C. external and internal obliques
D. erector spinae

9. In addition to the deltoid, which muscle functions to extend the elbow during a military press?

   A. Triceps B. Supra spinatus
   C. Trapezius D. Biceps

10. The latissimus dorsi's PRIMARY function includes

    A. extension B. adduction
    C. medial rotation D. all of the above

11. The MOST effective position for work is when the bone-muscle angle is closest to _____ degrees.

    A. 160 B. 180 C. 120 D. 90

12. Shoulder shrugs with resistance will utilize the

    A. rhomboids B. latissimus dorsi
    C. trapezius D. all of the above

13. A pivot joint responsible for supination-pronation of the forearm is the

    A. elbow B. wrist
    C. radioulnar D. none of the above

14. Rotation of the foot to the outside so the plantar surface tends to face away from the midline of the body is called

    A. inversion B. eversion
    C. supination D. pronation

15. The muscles involved in shoulder adduction are
    I. pectoralis major
    II. latissimus dorsi
    III. middle deltoid
    The CORRECT answer is:

    A. I and II B. II only
    C. I and III D. II and III

16. The gluteus maximus is responsible for
    I. medial rotation
    II. hip extension.
    III. hip flexion
    IV. lateral rotation
    The CORRECT answer is:

    A. I and II B. I, III, and IV
    C. II and III D. II and IV

17. According to _____, bone is capable of adjusting its strength in proportion to the amount of stress placed on it.

    A. Collagen Law
    B. osteoporosis
    C. Wolff's Law
    D. the Amenorrheic Rule

18. Maintaining the natural curves of the back without flexion, extension, rotation, or excessive anterior pelvic tilt is referred to as

    A. neutral position
    B. base of support
    C. gravitational pull
    D. antigravity position

19. In a case of *impingement syndrome,* the performance of _____ should be restricted.

    A. side lateral raises
    B. military press
    C. pull downs
    D. bleep curls

20. If adductors and internal rotators are tight or scapular adductors are weak and overstretched, or pectoralis minor is tight, _____ may be exhibited.

    A. lordosis
    B. round-shouldered posture
    C. rotator cuff injury
    D. impingement syndrome

21. Blood flow through the heart is as follows:

    A. RA-RV-LA-LV
    B. LA-LV-RV-RA
    C. RA-biscuspid valves-RV-LV tricuspid v LA
    D. superior vena cava-RA, RV-pulmonary veins, CA-LV-lunges

22. The exchange of O_2 and CO_2 between the atmosphere and the blood within the capillaries in the lungs is called _____ respiration.

    A. internal   B. external   C. asthmatic   D. cellular

23. Which are rotation cuff muscles?

    A. Supraspinatus
    B. Subscapularis
    C. Teres minor
    D. All of the above

24. The internal oblique muscle fibers run

    A. anteriorly downward and toward the midline
    B. horizontally
    C. posteriorly downward
    D. vertically from pubis to rib cage

25. Nerve cells that carry impulses from the CNS to respond to perceived changes in the internal and external environment of the body are called _____ cells.

    A. motor nerve
    B. sensory nerve
    C. receptor
    D. all of the above

KEY (CORRECT ANSWERS)

1. C
2. A
3. C
4. B
5. D

6. A
7. D
8. C
9. A
10. D

11. D
12. C
13. C
14. B
15. A

16. D
17. C
18. A
19. B
20. B

21. D
22. B
23. D
24. C
25. A

TEST 2

DIRECTIONS: Each question or incomplete statement is followed by several suggested answers or completions. Select the one that BEST answers the question or completes the statement. *PRINT THE LETTER OF THE CORRECT ANSWER IN THE SPACE AT THE RIGHT.*

1. Choose the correct pair of the muscle tissue matched with the appropriate contraction: 1.____
    I. Skeletal - voluntary
    II. Cardiac - voluntary
    III. Visceral - voluntary
   The CORRECT answer is:

   A. I *only*   B. I and II
   C. II and III   D. I, II, and III

2. Which of the following is CORRECT? 2.____
   _____ cervical, _____ thoracic, _____ lumbar, _____ .

   A. 7; 5; 7; 5 coccyx
   B. 5; 12; 7; 5 coccyx
   C. 7; 12; 5; 5 sacral, 4 coccyx
   D. 12; 7; 7; 5 sacral fused

3. Within the sagittal plane flexion and extension occurrences, _____ the angle between 3.____
   the articulating bones.
    I. flexion decreases
    II. flexion increases
    III. extension decreases
    IV. extension increases
   The CORRECT answer is:

   A. II *only*   B. II and III *only*
   C. I and III *only*   D. I and IV *only*

4. Of the joint structures below, the one that names NO joint cavity and includes all of the 4.____
   joints where bones are held together by fibrous connective tissue is

   A. fibrous joints   B. synovial joints
   C. cartilaginous joints   D. all skeletal articulations

5. Which of the following muscles are bi-articulate? 5.____

   A. Vastus medius   B. Soleus
   C. Hamstring muscles   D. All of the above

Questions 6-11.

DIRECTIONS: In Questions 6 through 11, refer to the following diagram and write the label of the numbered structure in the appropriate space at the right.

5

2 (#2)

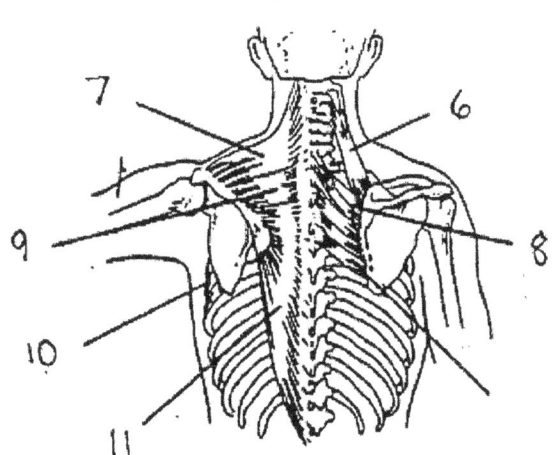

6.____
7.____
8.____
9.____
10.____
11.____

Questions 12-14.

DIRECTIONS: In Questions 12 through 14, refer to the following diagram and write the label of the numbered structure in the appropriate space at the right.

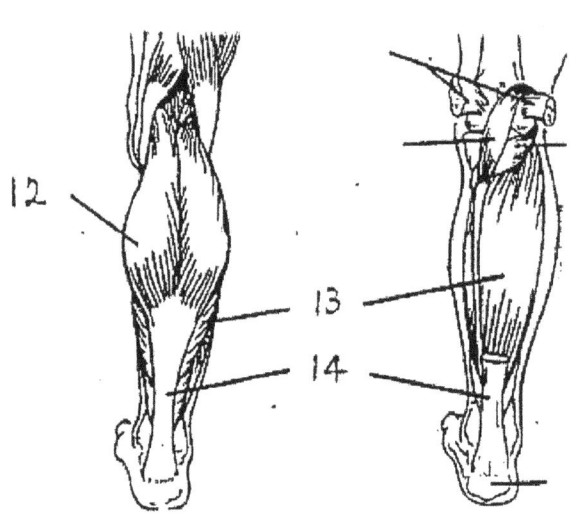

12.____
13.____
14.____

Questions 15-25.

DIRECTIONS: In Questions 15 through 25, refer to the following diagram and write the label of the numbered structure in the appropriate space at the right.

3 (#2)

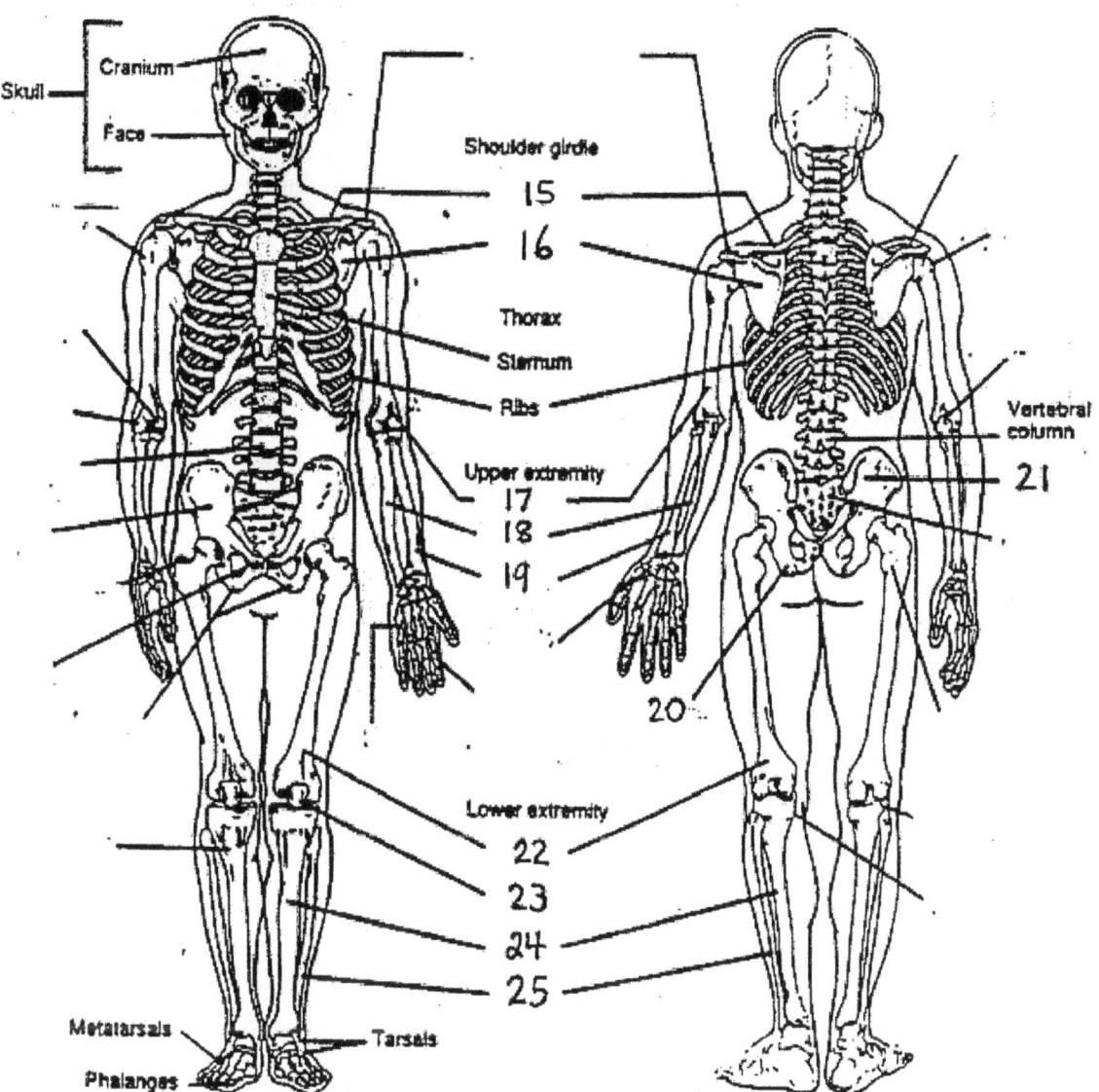

15. ____
16. ____
17. ____
18. ____
19. ____
20. ____
21. ____
22. ____
23. ____
24. ____
25. ____

4 (#2)

KEY (CORRECT ANSWERS)

1. B
2. C
3. D
4. A
5. C

6. levatator scapulae
7. upper trapezius
8. rhomboids
9. middle trapezius
10. serratus anterior

11. lower trapezius
12. gastroenciumis
13. soleus
14. achilles tendon
15. clavicle
16. scapula
17. humerus
18. ulna
19. radius
20. ishium

21. illium
22. femur
23. patella
24. tibia
25. fibula

MUSCULOSKELETAL SYSTEM & INJURIES
EXAMINATION SECTION
TEST 1

DIRECTIONS: Each question or incomplete statement is followed by several suggested answers or completions. Select the one that BEST answers the question or completes the statement. *PRINT THE LETTER OF THE CORRECT ANSWER IN THE SPACE AT THE RIGHT.*

1. All of the following are part of the musculoskeletal system EXCEPT 1.___

    A. bones and muscles
    B. ligaments and tendons
    C. spleen and liver
    D. cartilage

2. The musculoskeletal system is NOT responsible for 2.___

    A. support and shape
    B. clearance of waste products
    C. protection and locomotion
    D. production of red blood cells

3. The spinal column performs all of the following functions EXCEPT 3.___

    A. protect the spinal cord
    B. support the head and trunk
    C. carry impulses from the brain to the other parts of the body
    D. more than one but not all of the above

4. All of the following correlations of rate, area, and cause of incidence are true regarding spinal column injury EXCEPT: 4.___

    A. low; cervical and lumbar spine; good support
    B. high; cervical and lumbar spine; lack of support
    C. low; thoracic spine; support of the ribs
    D. low; sacrum; support of the pelvis

5. Regarding the rib cage, it is NOT true that the 5.___

    A. upper seven pairs of ribs are joined in front by the sternum
    B. next three pairs of ribs are joined by cartilage attached to the sternum
    C. eleventh and twelfth pairs of ribs have no front attachment
    D. clavicle or collarbone does not support the sternum

6. Major components of joints include all of the following EXCEPT 6.___

    A. bone ends covered with articular cartilage
    B. synovial membrane which produces a lubricating fluid
    C. capsules in a thin elastic layer
    D. ligaments or bands of connective tissue that bind the bones together, allowing some flexibility

7. Ball and socket joints provide a range of motion which is

   A. restricted to the left side only of the joint
   B. restricted only to the right side of the joint
   C. wide in all directions
   D. all of the above

8. Pelvis hip bones consist of all of the following EXCEPT the

   A. ileum   B. carpals   C. ischium   D. pubis

9. The functions of skeletal muscles do NOT include

   A. only exerting force by contracting
   B. working in pairs
   C. not moving the bones
   D. tendons attaching the muscles to the bones

10. Among the different types of muscles in the body is (are) _____ muscles.

    A. voluntary
    B. involuntary
    C. cardiac
    D. all of the above

11. When a bone is broken at the point of impact, it is called a

    A. twisting injury
    B. direct injury
    C. fatigue fracture
    D. none of the above

12. A fracture occurring at some distance from the impact is referred to as a(n)

    A. pathologic fracture
    B. direct injury
    C. indirect injury
    D. twisting injury

13. Joints, such as those between the bones of the hand, which allow very subtle and delicate movement are called _____ joints.

    A. ball and socket
    B. gliding
    C. pivot
    D. all of the above

14. Joints, such as those of the fingers, which permit flexion and extension are called _____ joints.

    A. hinge
    B. pivot
    C. gliding
    D. ball and socket

15. The _____ is a bone covered by a membrane.

    A. synovial membrane
    B. pericardium
    C. periosteum
    D. all of the above

16. The strength and hardness of bone is due PRIMARILY to

    A. calcium
    B. sodium
    C. phosphorus
    D. A and C *only*

17. Smooth or involuntary muscle mostly constitutes the muscle of the internal organs. Such muscle can be found in the walls of the

    A. urinary bladder
    B. blood vessels
    C. digestive system
    D. all of the above

18. Muscle contraction requires energy, which is derived from the metabolism of glucose and results in the production of

    A. galactose
    B. lactic acid
    C. lactose
    D. none of the above

19. Of the following injuries, which one MOST frequently occurs in association with pelvic fracture?

    A. Urinary bladder injury
    B. Femoral head dislocation
    C. Popliteal artery rupture
    D. None of the above

20. The fracture which occurs in children whose bones are still pliable, is a break straight across the bone, and goes only part-way through the bone is called _____ fracture.

    A. spiral
    B. greenstick
    C. impacted
    D. comminuted

21. The injuries in which ligaments are partially torn, usually as a result of the sudden twisting of a joint beyond its normal range of motion, are

    A. strains
    B. sprains
    C. dislocations
    D. none of the above

22. Soft tissue injuries or muscle spasms around a joint characterized by pain on active movement are called

    A. strains
    B. sprains
    C. dislocations
    D. A and B *only*

23. The pre-hospital management of a victim with anterior dislocation of the sternoclavicular joint would MOST likely include a(n)

    A. cold pack sling
    B. air splint
    C. pad axilla
    D. none of the above

24. A victim who sustained a clavicle fracture as a result of a direct blow would MOST likely receive the pre-hospital treatment of a(n)

    A. cold pack sling and swath
    B. air splint
    C. board splint
    D. none of the above

Questions 25-30.

DIRECTIONS: In Questions 25 through 30, match the numbered description with the lettered classification of fracture, listed in the column below, which it BEST describes. Place the letter of the CORRECT answer in the appropriate space at the right.

CLASSIFICATION OF FRACTURES
- A. Transverse
- B. Spiral
- C. Impacted
- D. Comminuted
- E. Oblique
- F. Greenstick

25. Ends of broken bones are jammed into each other. 25.____

26. Break forms an angle to the shaft. 26.____

27. Break is straight across the shaft of a bone. 27.____

28. Bone is fragmented. 28.____

29. Fracture has the appearance of a spring; break twists around the shaft of the bone. 29.____

30. Fracture is incomplete and common in children whose bones are still soft and pliable. 30.____

KEY (CORRECT ANSWERS)

1.	C	16.	D
2.	B	17.	D
3.	C	18.	B
4.	A	19.	A
5.	D	20.	B
6.	C	21.	B
7.	C	22.	A
8.	B	23.	D
9.	C	24.	C
10.	D	25.	C
11.	B	26.	E
12.	C	27.	A
13.	B	28.	D
14.	A	29.	B
15.	C	30.	F

TEST 2

DIRECTIONS: Each question or incomplete statement is followed by several suggested answers or completions. Select the one that BEST answers the question or completes the statement. *PRINT THE LETTER OF THE CORRECT ANSWER IN THE SPACE AT THE RIGHT.*

1. To immobilize a fracture of the _____, use a _____. 1._____

    A. hip; full backboard
    B. foot or ankle; pillow
    C. shoulder or clavicle; sling or swathe
    D. all of the above

2. The MAJOR complication of anterior dislocation of the shoulder is _____ injury. 2._____

    A. radial damage   B. axillary nerve
    C. subclavian artery   D. all of the above

3. Possible complications of posterior dislocation of the sternoclavicular joint include 3._____

    A. damage to trachea   B. damage to esophagus
    C. pneumothorax   D. all of the above

4. One possible complication of a clavicular fracture may be 4._____

    A. subclavian artery injury
    B. axillary artery injury
    C. Volk-Mannis ischemic contracture
    D. none of the above

5. A victim involved in a motor vehicle accident sustained a fracture of the shaft of the humerus. He has ecchymosis, swelling and deformity of the area. 5._____
Among the complications he may encounter is _____ nerve injury.

    A. ulner   B. radial
    C. median   D. all of the above

6. Pre-hospital treatment of a fracture of the shaft of the humerus includes 6._____

    A. sling and swathe   B. padded board splint
    C. hot pack   D. A and B *only*

7. The MOST likely complication of an elbow fracture (e.g., skateboard injury) is 7._____

    A. Volk-Mannis ischemic contracture
    B. shock
    C. wrist drop
    D. A and C *only*

8. A victim who falls on a hyperextended arm and develops locked painful elbow is MOST likely to develop which of the following complications? 8._____

    A. Ulner nerve injury
    B. Vascular injury
    C. Associated injuries to the rib
    D. All of the above

9. Pre-hospital management of a forearm fracture would include

   A. air splint
   B. padded board splint
   C. all of the above
   D. none of the above

10. The signs and symptoms of dislocation include

    A. an obvious deformity of the joint
    B. swelling at the joint and pain which increases with movement
    C. loss of use of the joint or complaint of a locked or frozen joint
    D. all of the above

11. The MOST common symptom of strain is

    A. pain
    B. discoloration
    C. hematoma
    D. all of the above

12. Among the common symptoms of a sprain is

    A. swelling
    B. discoloration
    C. pain on movement
    D. all of the above

13. Of the following, the FIRST priority of care is for fractures of the

    A. spine
    B. head, rib cage, and pelvis
    C. extremities
    D. none of the above

14. When a bone is broken or dislocated, the process of _____ supplies a substitute support and immobilization to the bone.

    A. traction
    B. splinting
    C. all of the above
    D. none of the above

15. A _____ fracture is the fracture of the wrist that gives a silverfork appearance.

    A. boxer's
    B. colles
    C. nightstick
    D. none of the above

16. A garden spade deformity occurs when a victim

    A. falls on his outstretched hand
    B. falls on his extended wrist
    C. gets his hand slammed in a car door
    D. all of the above

17. General treatment of injuries to the lower extremities includes

    A. pulse and nerve function assessment
    B. manual traction
    C. spinal protection
    D. all of the above

Questions 18-19.

DIRECTIONS: Questions 18 and 19 are to be answered on the basis of the following information.

A victim is hit by a car and suffers hematoma of the scrotum. He is complaining of pain on compression of the iliac wings. You suspect a pelvic fracture.

18. Pre-hospital treatment, after the ABCs, may include 18.___

    A. mast
    B. backboard
    C. IV fluid
    D. all of the above

19. Among the possible complications of the above patient's condition is 19.___

    A. shock
    B. bladder or urethra injury
    C. associated spinal injury
    D. all of the above

20. A victim who has a dislocated knee may also have 20.___

    A. shock
    B. sciatic nerve injury
    C. popliteal artery injury
    D. all of the above

21. A victim who sustained an angulated tibia and fibula fracture is at high risk of developing 21.___

    A. shock
    B. compartment syndrome
    C. an associated lumbar spine fracture
    D. all of the above

22. All of the following sets of bones are part of the hand EXCEPT 22.___

    A. carpals
    B. metatarsals
    C. metacarpals
    D. phalanges

23. A fracture of the fifth metacarpal MOST typically occurs in 23.___

    A. boxers
    B. duelers
    C. wrestlers
    D. none of the above

24. The proximal bony projection of the ulna at the elbow which constitutes the *funny bone* is called the 24.___

    A. olecranon
    B. patella
    C. humerus
    D. malleolus

25. The tough bands of tissue connecting bone to bone around a joint or supporting internal organs within the body are called 25.___

    A. synovial joints
    B. ligaments
    C. tendons
    D. malleolus

Questions 26-30.

DIRECTIONS: In Questions 26 through 30, match the numbered description with the lettered part of the musculoskeletal system, listed in Column I, which it BEST describes. Place the letter of the CORRECT answer in the appropriate space at the right.

COLUMN I
A. Axial skeleton
B. Appendicular skeleton
C. Tendon
D. Tibia
E. Trochanter

26. The part of the skeleton comprising the upper and lower extremities 26.___

27. The part of the skeleton comprising the skull, spinal column and rib cage 27.___

28. Either of the two processes below the neck of the femur 28.___

29. The fibrous portion of muscle that attaches to bone 29.___

30. The shin bone 30.___

Questions 31-35.

DIRECTIONS: In Questions 31 through 35, match the numbered description with the lettered part of the musculoskeletal system, listed in Column I, which it BEST describes. Place the letter of the CORRECT answer in the appropriate space at the right.

COLUMN I
A. Diaphysis
B. Epiphysis
C. Periosteum
D. Acetabulum
E. Metatarsals

31. Strong, white, fibrous material which covers the bone 31.___

32. Portion of spongy bone covered with compact bone 32.___

33. Central shaft of a long bone composed of compact bone 33.___

34. Foot bones 34.___

35. Cup-shaped cavity in which the rounded head of the femur rotates 35.___

KEY (CORRECT ANSWERS)

1.	D	16.	B
2.	B	17.	D
3.	D	18.	D
4.	A	19.	D
5.	B	20.	C
6.	D	21.	B
7.	A	22.	B
8.	B	23.	A
9.	C	24.	A
10.	D	25.	B
11.	A	26.	B
12.	D	27.	A
13.	A	28.	E
14.	B	29.	C
15.	B	30.	D

31. C
32. B
33. A
34. E
35. D

EXAMINATION SECTION
TEST 1

DIRECTIONS: Each question or incomplete statement is followed by several suggested answers or completions. Select the one that BEST answers the question or completes the statement. *PRINT THE LETTER OF THE CORRECT ANSWER IN THE SPACE AT THE RIGHT.*

1. An impairment whose underlying cause includes both direct and indirect effects of the original pathology or insult is called a(n) 1.____

    A. handicap
    B. impairment
    C. composite impairment
    D. ailment
    E. none of the above

2. The social disadvantage that results when an impairment or disability prevents an individual from fulfilling his or her normal role is called a(n) 2.____

    A. handicap
    B. impairment
    C. disability
    D. indirect impairment
    E. sick

3. Which of the following phases characterizes a problem-oriented, organized approach to the patient-treatment process? 3.____

    A. Formation of database
    B. Identification of a specific problem list
    C. Identification of a specific treatment plan
    D. Evaluation of the effectiveness of treatment plans
    E. All of the above

4. Any loss or abnormality of anatomic, physiologic, or psychologic structure or function is known as a(n) 4.____

    A. handicap
    B. disability
    C. impairment
    D. sickness
    E. indirect impairment

5. Alignment of one's inner needs with the realities of personal capabilities and/or environments is termed 5.____

    A. adaptation
    B. adjustment
    C. deviation
    D. coping
    E. none of the above

6. The ongoing active process through which an individual adjusts to changing environmental life situations is 6.____

    A. acceptance
    B. adjustment
    C. adaptation
    D. hostility
    E. coping

7. Which of the following is the process through which individuals deal with the variety of social and environmental factors encountered in life? 7.____

    A. Adaptation
    B. Adjustment
    C. Coping
    D. Deviation
    E. Denial

19

8. Cognition is the process by which an organism becomes knowledgeable. It is influenced by one's

   A. personality characteristics
   B. emotional factors
   C. subjectivity
   D. all of the above
   E. none of the above

9. Which of the following is characterized by emotional instability manifested by alterations or fluctuations in emotional state?

   A. Lability
   B. Cognition
   C. Hostility
   D. Patient role
   E. Denial

10. The state of exaggerated feelings of depression often accompanied by anxiety is called

    A. euphoria
    B. dysuria
    C. dysphoria
    D. aphoria
    E. maladaptation

11. A _____ consists of specified clusters of behaviors and expectations attached to each distinct, identified relationship to another person or persons.

    A. script
    B. role
    C. self-image
    D. defense
    E. perception

12. A set of moral norms adopted by a professional group to direct value-laden choices in a way consistent with professional responsibility is called

    A. confidentiality
    B. empathy
    C. compassion
    D. code of ethics
    E. justice

13. Which of the following is NOT a stage of the process known as *empathy*?

    A. Identification with another's experience
    B. A shared experience with another person
    C. A reclaiming of one's individuality separate from the shared moment
    D. Feeling at one with another's feelings
    E. None of the above

14. Indifference is characterized by all of the following EXCEPT

    A. lack of interest
    B. lack of concern
    C. aloofness
    D. detachment
    E. none of the above

15. Vital signs, also referred to as cardinal signs, GENERALLY include

    A. temperature
    B. pulse
    C. respiration
    D. blood pressure
    E. all of the above

16. The purposes of obtaining information related to vital signs include all of the following EXCEPT

    A. establishing a database of values for an individual patient
    B. assessing patient's response to treatment
    C. assisting in discharge planning and future follow-up
    D. assisting in goal setting and treatment planning
    E. assessing effectiveness of treatment

17. The thermoreceptors provide input to the temperature-regulating center, located in the

    A. thalamus
    B. hypothalamus
    C. pons
    D. hypophysis
    E. midbrain

18. All of the following are effector organs/systems which function either to increase or to dissipate body heat EXCEPT

    A. vascular system
    B. metabolic system
    C. urinary system
    D. musculoskeletal system
    E. sweat glands

19. The one of the following that is NOT a description of a heat conservation and production mechanism is

    A. vasoconstriction of blood vessels
    B. decrease in sweat gland activity
    C. decreased cellular metabolism
    D. shivering
    E. increased output of thyroxine

20. All of the following are mechanisms by which the human body dissipates heat EXCEPT

    A. conservation
    B. evaporation
    C. conduction
    D. convection
    E. radiation

21. All of the following are symptoms of hypothermia EXCEPT

    A. decreased pulse
    B. drowsiness
    C. decreased respiration
    D. shivering
    E. cyanosis

22. The symptoms of hyperpyrexia do NOT include

    A. general malaise
    B. disorientation
    C. confusion
    D. convulsions
    E. coma

23. All of the following hormones are involved in regulation of temperature EXCEPT

    A. norepinephrine
    B. epinephrine
    C. thyroxine
    D. parathyroid
    E. none of the above

24. Body temperature is influenced by

    A. time of day
    B. age
    C. emotions
    D. exercise
    E. all of the above

25. Lower body temperatures in elderly populations are associated with

    A. lower metabolic rate
    B. decreased subcutaneous tissue mass
    C. decreased physical activity level
    D. inadequate diet
    E. all of the above

KEY (CORRECT ANSWERS)

1.	C	11.	B
2.	A	12.	D
3.	E	13.	D
4.	C	14.	E
5.	B	15.	E
6.	C	16.	C
7.	C	17.	B
8.	D	18.	C
9.	A	19.	C
10.	C	20.	A

21. D
22. A
23. D
24. E
25. E

TEST 2

DIRECTIONS: Each question or incomplete statement is followed by several suggested answers or completions. Select the one that BEST answers the question or completes the statement. *PRINT THE LETTER OF THE CORRECT ANSWER IN THE SPACE AT THE RIGHT.*

1. All of the following are contraindications for taking a temperature orally EXCEPT   1.____

    A. patients with dyspnea
    B. surgical procedures involving mouth and throat
    C. very young children
    D. adolescents
    E. delirious patients

2. Several factors are particularly important when considering pulse rate, such as   2.____

    A. age
    B. sex
    C. emotions
    D. exercise
    E. all of the above

3. When there is a DECREASED amplitude of pressure wave with inspiration and a return to full amplitude on expiration, it is called _____ pulse.   3.____

    A. bounding
    B. thready
    C. paradoxical
    D. alternating
    E. bigeminal

4. The respiratory muscles are controlled by motor nerves, whose cell bodies are located in the   4.____

    A. hypothalamus
    B. thalamus
    C. pons and medulla
    D. putamen
    E. hypophysis

5. Respiration is influenced by   5.____

    A. age
    B. body size
    C. stature
    D. exercise
    E. all of the above

6. A respiratory pattern that alternates between periods of apnea and hyperpnea is called Biot's respiration.
It is associated with   6.____

    A. fever
    B. hypotension
    C. emphysema
    D. increased intracranial pressure
    E. ketoacidosis

7. A gasping, labored pattern with both increased rate and depth, that is, rapid and deep respirations without pauses, is called   7.____

    A. Biot's respiration
    B. Kussmaul's respiration
    C. apneustic respiration
    D. Cheyne-Stokes breathing
    E. apnea

8. Which of the following respiratory sounds is described as a deep inspiration followed by a prolonged, audible expiration?

    A. Wheezing   B. Stridor   C. Rales
    D. Sigh   E. Snoring

9. A respiratory pattern characterized by a gradual increase in rate and depth, followed by a gradual decrease with a period of apnea occurring between cycles, is called

    A. Cheyne-Stokes respiration
    B. Kussmaul's breathing
    C. apneustic breathing
    D. paradoxical breathing
    E. Biot's respiration

10. Cheyne-Stokes respiration is often associated with

    A. severe congestive heart failure
    B. renal failure
    C. drug overdose
    D. meningitis
    E. all of the above

11. The NORMAL range of systolic blood pressure for an adult is _____ mmHg.

    A. 105-125   B. 100-115
    C. 110-140   D. 140-160
    E. none of the above

12. Which of the following factors influences blood pressure?

    A. Blood volume   B. Elasticity of arteries
    C. Cardiac output   D. Valsalva maneuver
    E. All of the above

13. Fluctuations in temperature above normal without returning to normal between fluctuations is termed _____ fever.

    A. intermittent   B. relapsing   C. remittent
    D. sustained   E. diurnal

14. An attempt to exhale forcibly with the glottis, nose, and mouth closed, causing increased intrathoracic pressure, is known as _____ maneuver.

    A. Heimlich   B. valsalva   C. Bracht's
    D. McDonald's   E. Kocher

15. The tissues of the body involved in musculoskeletal function/dysfunction are called *soft tissues* and consist of all of the following EXCEPT the

    A. dermis   B. muscles   C. tendons
    D. bone   E. ligaments

16. Soft tissue dysfunction produces all of the following categories of problems which form the basis of interventions in physical therapy EXCEPT

    A. pain   B. depression   C. contracture
    D. instability   E. weakness

17. During the examination process, the physical therapist controls the variables by applying   17.____
    an external force while palpating and observing the response of the tissues. The external
    force can be modified by altering the

    A. magnitude of force
    B. duration of force application
    C. velocity of application
    D. frequency of application
    E. all of the above

18. A load that pushes the fibers of a material together along its long axis is called   18.____

    A. stress   B. strain   C. compression
    D. tension   E. torsion

19. When an internal load imposed by forces acting in opposite directions results in the ten-   19.____
    dency to elongate, or in the actual elongation of, the fibers in a material, it is termed

    A. stress   B. strain   C. compression
    D. tension   E. torsion

20. Which of the following characteristics of resistance during passive motion should be con-   20.____
    sidered while monitoring a patient's report of pain?
    The

    A. presence of pain accompanying the resistance
    B. point in the range where resistance is felt
    C. type of resistance
    D. all of the above
    E. none of the above

21. End-feel type of resistance is felt by the examiner when there is a passive stretching of a   21.____
    joint and its associated soft tissues.
    All of the following are normal end-feels EXCEPT

    A. boggy   B. soft
    C. firm   D. hard
    E. none of the above

22. Of the following joint motions, only _____ is NOT an example of a normal end-feel.   22.____

    A. elbow extension
    B. displaced meniscus at the tibiofemoral joint
    C. elbow and knee flexion
    D. forearm supination
    E. shoulder and hip rotation

23. All of the following are examples of pathologic end-feels EXCEPT   23.____

    A. muscle spasm   B. hard   C. empty
    D. capsular   E. laxity

24. Which of the following is NOT a pattern of pain and strength providing additional information regarding the tissue?
    _____ indicates _____.
    A. Painful and strong; minor lesion
    B. Painful and weak; minor lesion
    C. Painful and weak; lesion of neurologic origin
    D. Painful and weak; major lesion
    E. Painless and strong; normal function

25. The components of the screening examination for normal and abnormal findings of the musculoskeletal and peripheral neurologic systems include
    A. vital signs
    B. mental status
    C. inspection
    D. neurologic assessment
    E. all of the above

KEY (CORRECT ANSWERS)

1.	D	11.	C
2.	E	12.	E
3.	C	13.	C
4.	C	14.	B
5.	E	15.	D
6.	D	16.	B
7.	B	17.	E
8.	D	18.	C
9.	A	19.	D
10.	E	20.	D

21. A
22. B
23. B
24. B
25. E

EXAMINATION SECTION
TEST 1

DIRECTIONS: Each question or incomplete statement is followed by several suggested answers or completions. Select the one that BEST answers the question or completes the statement. *PRINT THE LETTER OF THE CORRECT ANSWER IN THE SPACE AT THE RIGHT.*

1. All of the following should be checked during inspection while performing a musculoskeletal exam EXCEPT

    A. posture
    B. joint effusion
    C. soft tissue edema
    D. skin condition
    E. none of the above

    1._____

2. A 32-year-old man is referred to you for physiotherapy. He is complaining of bilateral pain in his biceps muscles. The involved nerve is the _____ nerve.

    A. radial
    B. ulnar
    C. scapular
    D. musculocutaneous
    E. long thoracic

    2._____

3. An eight-year-old boy is complaining of elbow pain on the right side after a fall on his right side. He cannot flex his right elbow. The muscle MOST likely affected is the

    A. deltoid
    B. biceps
    C. triceps
    D. musculocutaneous
    E. flexor carpi ulnaris

    3._____

4. While performing neurological assessment for a musculoskeletal problem in an 80-year-old man, which of the following forms of sensation should be checked?

    A. Superficial tactile
    B. Superficial pain
    C. Temperature
    D. Vibration
    E. All of the above

    4._____

5. A 28-year-old man comes to you for evaluation. He was hit by a baseball bat on his right arm, which presented with swelling and pain. On examination, you find a soft tissue lesion without a mechanical deficit.
Your treatment strategy for this patient should be to

    A. promote tissue nutrition
    B. alter mechanical tissue load
    C. prevent formation of soft tissue restrictions or insufficiency
    D. promote motor control
    E. all of the above

    5._____

6. All of the following are cutaneous sensory receptors EXCEPT

    A. Golgi tendon organs
    B. Ruffini's endings
    C. Kraus's end-bulbs
    D. Merkel's disks
    E. Meissner's corpuscles

    6._____

7. The _____ system carries the fibers for temperature sense.

    A. anterior spinothalamic
    B. posterior spinothalamic
    C. lateral spinothalamic
    D. spinoarticular
    E. medial lemniscal

8. The one of the following sensations that is NOT transmitted by the dorsal column-medial lemniscal system is

    A. stereognosis
    B. temperature
    C. barognosis
    D. graphesthesia
    E. two-point discrimination

9. A 25-year-old man comes into the office complaining of inability to recognize the form and shape of objects by touch.
    The MOST likely diagnosis is

    A. abaragnosis
    B. allesthesia
    C. astereognosis
    D. causalgia
    E. thalamic syndrome

10. The function of the cerebellum is

    A. coordination of motor activity
    B. equilibrium
    C. muscle tone
    D. all of the above
    E. none of the above

11. Which of the following clinical signs are manifestations of cerebellar dysfunction or lesions?

    A. Hypotonia
    B. Dysmetria
    C. Tremors
    D. Nystagmus
    E. All of the above

12. A martial arts student comes to the physician complaining of having problems judging the range of kick or punch. This is a cerebellar dysfunction known as

    A. dysdiadochokinesia
    B. dysmetria
    C. ataxia
    D. rebound phenomenon
    E. hypotonia

13. Impaired ability to perform rapid alternating movements is called

    A. dysdiadochokinesia
    B. dysmetria
    C. dysarthria
    D. tremors
    E. asthenia

14. All of the following are manifestations of cerebellar lesions EXCEPT

    A. disorders of gait
    B. ataxia
    C. rigidity
    D. dysarthria
    E. asthenia

15. The basal ganglia are a group of nuclei located at the base of the cerebral cortex. All of the following are true basal ganglia nuclei EXCEPT

    A. caudate
    B. substancia nigra
    C. putamen
    D. globus pallidus
    E. none of the above

16. A lesion of the contralateral subthalamic nucleus manifests as a sudden, jerky, forceful, wild, flailing motion of the arm and leg of one side of the body called

    A. athetosis
    B. chorea
    C. hemiballismus
    D. choreoathetosis
    E. dystonia

17. All of the following are clinical manifestations of lesions of the basal ganglia EXCEPT

    A. bradykinesia
    B. chorea
    C. athetosis
    D. nystagmus
    E. rigidity

18. Changes in coordinated movement that occur with age do NOT include

    A. decreased strength
    B. slowed reaction time
    C. loss of flexibility
    D. no postural abnormality
    E. impaired balance

19. All of the following are nonequilibrium coordination tests EXCEPT

    A. standing on one foot
    B. finger to finger
    C. alternate nose to finger
    D. finger to nose
    E. finger opposition

20. A 35-year-old man comes to the office with complaints of choreiform movements, disturbance of tone, posture, and gait, and dementia. A diagnosis of Huntington's disease is made.
    All of the following are characteristics of this condition EXCEPT

    A. degenerative disease of basal ganglia and cerebral cortex
    B. autosomal dominant
    C. onset is usually after age 15
    D. frequently fatal within 5-15 years after onset
    E. none of the above

21. All of the following are abnormalities of muscle tone EXCEPT

    A. spasticity
    B. rigidity
    C. end-feel
    D. flaccidity
    E. dystonia

22. Brain stem lesions can produce either decerebrate or decorticate rigidity. Decerebrate rigidity is defined as

    A. rachetlike response to passive movement
    B. decreased or absent muscle tone
    C. impaired or disordered tone

D. sustained contraction and posturing of the trunk and limbs in a position of full extension
E. characteristic feel each specific joint has at the end of range of motion

23. Which of the following nerves are involved in tricep reflex?   23._____
    A. C_5 and C_6
    B. C_6 and C_7
    C. Trigeminal
    D. C_7 and C_8
    E. C_4 and C_5

24. Of the following, only the _____ reflex is NOT a primitive spinal reflex.   24._____
    A. flexor withdrawal
    B. moro
    C. asymmetric tonic neck
    D. grasp
    E. startle

25. The tonic/brainstem reflexes include the _____ reflex.   25._____
    A. asymmetric tonic neck
    B. symmetric tonic neck
    C. symmetric tonic labrynthine
    D. positive supporting
    E. all of the above

KEY (CORRECT ANSWERS)

1. E		11. E	
2. D		12. B	
3. B		13. A	
4. E		14. C	
5. E		15. B	
6. A		16. C	
7. C		17. D	
8. B		18. D	
9. C		19. A	
10. D		20. C	

21. C
22. D
23. D
24. C
25. E

TEST 2

DIRECTIONS: Each question or incomplete statement is followed by several suggested answers or completions. Select the one that BEST answers the question or completes the statement. *PRINT THE LETTER OF THE CORRECT ANSWER IN THE SPACE AT THE RIGHT.*

1. A rachetlike response to passive movement characterized by an alternate letting go and increasing resistance to movement is known as cogwheel rigidity.
   Cogwheel rigidity is COMMONLY associated with

   A. upper motor neuron lesions
   B. lower motor neuron syndrome
   C. Parkinson's disease
   D. Huntington's disease
   E. choreoathetosis

1._____

2. While testing deep tendon reflexes, the patient is asked to hook together the fingers of the hands and attempt to pull them apart. While this pressure is maintained, reflexes are checked.
   This maneuver is called

   A. Jendrassik maneuver   B. valsalva maneuver
   C. Heimlich maneuver   D. McDonald's maneuver
   E. opostholonus

2._____

3. One of the MOST common chronic lung diseases for which pulmonary rehabilitation is rendered is

   A. pneumonia
   B. cystic fibrosis
   C. bronchiectasis
   D. chronic obstructive pulmonary disease
   E. tuberculosis

3._____

4. At full inspiration, the lungs contain their maximum amount of gas, called total lung capacity.
   Total lung capacity consists of _____ volume.
      I. tidal
      II. inspiratory reserve
      III. expiratory reserve
      IV. residual
   The CORRECT answer is:

   A. I, II, III, IV   B. I, II, III
   C. II, III, IV   D. II, III
   E. I, IV

4._____

5. The MOST common chronic pulmonary disorder after chronic obstructive pulmonary disease is

   A. pneumonia   B. cystic fibrosis
   C. asthma   D. tuberculosis
   E. bronchiectasis

5._____

6. All of the following are involved in the pathophysiology of chronic obstructive pulmonary disease EXCEPT

   A. chronic inflammation
   B. excessive secretions
   C. bronchoconstriction
   D. hyperinflation
   E. atelectasis

7. Characteristics of chronic obstructive pulmonary disease do NOT include

   A. inspiratory wheezing
   B. cyanosis
   C. digital clubbing
   D. crackles
   E. dyspnea on exertion

8. A 60-year-old known smoker has been diagnosed with emphysema and bronchitis for the last ten years. Which of the following chest radiographic findings would you expect?

   A. Depressed and flattened hemidiaphragms
   B. Alteration in pulmonary vascular markings
   C. Hyperinflation of the thorax
   D. Increased anterioposterior diameter of the chest
   E. All of the above

9. Asthma is a clinical syndrome which is pathophysiologically characterized by all of the following EXCEPT

   A. bronchospasm
   B. infiltrate
   C. inflammation of the bronchial mucosa
   D. increased bronchial secretion
   E. increased resistance to air flow

10. _____ is/are NOT a possible cause of asthma.

    A. Genetic predisposition
    B. Environmental contributions
    C. Autonomic nervous system imbalance
    D. Bacterial infections
    E. Mucosal epithelial damage

11. All of the following are true of cystic fibrosis EXCEPT

    A. autosomal recessive trait
    B. more common in white children
    C. abnormally viscid secretion
    D. multiple organ systems affected
    E. none of the above

12. Signs of restrictive lung disease include

    A. rapid shallow breathing
    B. limited chest expansion
    C. crackles in lower lung field
    D. digital clubbing
    E. all of the above

13. An 80-year-old patient with chronic obstructive pulmonary disease is referred to you for rehabilitation.
    Your treatment goals for this patient should include trying to

    A. provide ongoing secretion removal to optimize respiration
    B. initiate exercise training to improve the present level of function
    C. promote self-management of pulmonary disease
    D. provide patient and family education
    E. all of the above

14. A determination of functional capacity is part of the assessment of a patient with pulmonary disease. A graded exercise test is used for this purpose.
    Indications for the termination of a graded exercise test include

    A. minimal shortness of breath
    B. a fall in PaO_2 of greater than 10 mmHg
    C. PaO_2 less than 65 mmHg
    D. cardiac arrhythmia
    E. a rise in $PaCO_2$ of greater than 5 mmHg

15. Exercise prescription for pulmonary rehabilitation incorporates

    A. mode
    B. intensity
    C. duration
    D. frequency
    E. all of the above

16. Which of the following techniques are COMMONLY used to prescribe and monitor exercise intensity during a pulmonary rehabilitation program?

    A. Heart rate
    B. Rate of perceived shortness of breath
    C. Metabolic energy expenditure
    D. All of the above
    E. None of the above

17. Although aerobic exercise training is integral to pulmonary rehabilitation, patients may require some other information to optimize their exercise capability and quality of life.
    Other essential components of pulmonary rehabilitation include

    A. secretion removal techniques
    B. ventilatory muscle training
    C. breathing re-education
    D. smoking cessation
    E. all of the above

18. All of the following are precautions for the use of the Trendelenburg position for postural drainage of bronchial secretions EXCEPT

    A. pulmonary edema
    B. axillofemoral bypass graft
    C. congestive heart failure
    D. hypertension
    E. recent food consumption

19. Precautions for the use of percussion and shaking for drainage of pulmonary secretions do NOT include

    A. hemoptysis
    B. coagulation disorders
    C. obesity
    D. fractured ribs
    E. flail chest

20. Of the following risk factors for the development of cardiovascular disease, the one that can be modified through lifestyle changes is

    A. high blood pressure
    B. high blood cholesterol
    C. cigarette smoking
    D. physical inactivity
    E. all of the above

21. A risk factor for the development of cardiovascular disease which can be changed is

    A. hereditary factors
    B. stress
    C. male sex
    D. increasing age
    E. none of the above

22. The ischemia that results from inadequate coronary blood flow causes depressed left ventricular function, shown on the EKG chiefly as

    A. ST segment elevation
    B. ST segment depression
    C. peaked T wave
    D. downslope T wave
    E. none of the above

23. Myocardial infarction is the death of myocardial tissue secondary to prolonged ischemia. All of the following enzymes are elevated in the serum of the patient with myocardial infarction EXCEPT

    A. creatine phosphokinase
    B. lactate dehydrogenase
    C. asparate amniotransferase
    D. alkaline phosphatase
    E. none of the above

24. The MOST common and life-threatening complication following myocardial infarction is

    A. congestive heart failure
    B. arrhythmias
    C. ventricular aneurysm
    D. mitral insufficiency
    E. cardiomegaly

25. All of the following are deconditioning effects of prolonged bedrest EXCEPT a(n)

    A. decrease in physical work capacity
    B. increase in the heart rate response to effort
    C. increase in circulation blood volume
    D. decrease in lung volume and vital capacity
    E. decrease in serum protein concentration

KEY (CORRECT ANSWERS)

1.	C	11.	E
2.	A	12.	E
3.	D	13.	E
4.	A	14.	D
5.	C	15.	E
6.	C	16.	D
7.	A	17.	E
8.	E	18.	B
9.	B	19.	C
10.	D	20.	E

21. B
22. B
23. D
24. B
25. C

EXAMINATION SECTION
TEST 1

DIRECTIONS: Each question or incomplete statement is followed by several suggested answers or completions. Select the one that BEST answers the question or completes the statement. *PRINT THE LETTER OF THE CORRECT ANSWER IN THE SPACE AT THE RIGHT.*

1. A 53-year-old patient is in the hospital and has undergone coronary artery bypass surgery. An inpatient exercise program is prescribed.
   Which of the following would indicate ABNORMAL response to exercise therapy?

   A. Increased heart rate above the prescribed limit
   B. Marked change in blood pressure with exercise
   C. Significant exertional dyspnea
   D. Incisional pain
   E. All of the above

   1.____

2. You are asked to evaluate a 47-year-old woman for possible outpatient exercise programs.
   Contraindications to entrance into such a program include

   A. unstable angina
   B. moderate to severe aortic stenosis
   C. recent embolism
   D. uncontrolled diabetes
   E. all of the above

   2.____

3. Specific exercise progressions within a program GENERALLY include _____ exercises.

   A. passive to active to resistive
   B. distal to intermediate to proximal joint
   C. extremity to trunk
   D. lying to sitting to standing
   E. all of the above

   3.____

4. The roles of a physical therapist in overseeing the exercise portion of a cardiac rehabilitation program consist of all of the following EXCEPT

   A. evaluating the physiologic responses to exercise and activity
   B. supervising the exercises and ambulation
   C. not charting the patient's progress and responses
   D. assisting in patient and family education
   E. preparing the patient for discharge

   4.____

5. During a cardiac rehabilitation program, exercise responses are NOT monitored by

   A. heart rate before, during, and after each exercise
   B. respiratory rate changes during exercise
   C. blood pressure before, during, and after each exercise
   D. electrocardiogram at rest during and after exercise
   E. none of the above

   5.____

6. While on cardiac rehabilitation, a 47-year-old patient is doing therapist-supervised exercises.
   Which of the following signs and symptoms in this patient during exercise would indicate IMMEDIATE termination of exercise?

   A. Persistent dyspnea
   B. Dizziness or confusion
   C. Anginal pain
   D. Severe leg claudication
   E. All of the above

7. All of the following are goals of patient and family education programs during cardiac rehabilitation EXCEPT

   A. improving understanding of coronary artery disease and its management
   B. modifying risk factors
   C. alleviating fears and anxieties so that the patient can assume some responsibility for health care
   D. teaching cardiopulmonary resuscitation to a family member
   E. none of the above

8. A 73-year-old patient is going home, and you recommend an outpatient exercise program. The patient wants to know the advantages of this program.
   You should tell the patient that it would

   A. improve functional capacity
   B. progress towards full resumption of habitual and occupational activities
   C. promote positive lifestyle changes
   D. all of the above
   E. none of the above

9. The heart rate is used to prescribe and monitor exercise intensity, but can NOT be used to prescribe safe workloads in

   A. isometric exercise
   B. valsalva maneuver
   C. beta blocker medications
   D. pacemakers
   E. all of the above

10. All of the following are valid reasons to temporarily reduce or defer physical activity EXCEPT

    A. progression of cardiac disease
    B. orthopedic problem
    C. vitamin use
    D. dehydration
    E. emotional turmoil

11. Common causes of strokes do NOT include

    A. shock
    B. thrombus
    C. embolus
    D. hemorrhage due to aneurysm or trauma
    E. none of the above

12. The MOST common disease leading to or associated with stroke is   12.____

    A. coronary heart disease
    B. hypertension
    C. congestive heart failure
    D. peripheral arterial disease
    E. diabetes

13. The vertebral arteries, which are a branch of the sub-clavian artery, from both sides unite   13.____
    and give rise to the _____ artery.

    A. carotid   B. posterior communicating
    C. anterior communicating   D. basilar
    E. middle cerebral

14. Interruption of blood flow by atherosclerotic plaque occurs at certain sites of predilection.   14.____
    These sites GENERALLY include

    A. bifurcations   B. constrictions
    C. dilations   D. angulations
    E. all of the above

15. All of the following are supplied by the anterior cerebral artery EXCEPT the   15.____

    A. frontal lobe
    B. parietal lobe
    C. temporal lobe
    D. anterior internal capsule
    E. inferior caudate nucleus

16. A 59-year-old, known hypertensive patient had a stroke and now comes to you for reha-   16.____
    bilitation. He complains of memory and behavior impairments, aphasia, apraxia, and
    agraphia.
    The _____ artery was involved in his stroke.

    A. middle cerebral   B. anterior cerebral
    C. posterior cerebral   D. vertebral
    E. basilar

17. The MOST common site of strokes is the _____ artery.   17.____

    A. anterior cerebral   B. middle cerebral
    C. posterior cerebral   D. vertebral
    E. basilar

18. A communication disorder caused by brain damage and characterized by an impairment   18.____
    of language comprehension, formulation, and use is called

    A. agnosia   B. apraxia   C. aphasia
    D. ataxia   E. agraphia

19. Clinical manifestations of a stroke include

    A. impaired sensation
    B. impaired motor function
    C. alterations in tone
    D. speech and language disorders
    E. all of the above

20. All of the following are secondary impairments after a stroke EXCEPT

    A. psychological problems
    B. deep venous thrombosis
    C. shoulder pain
    D. increased sense of humor
    E. pain

21. While planning rehabilitative management for a neurologically impaired patient, the assessment should include

    A. mental status
    B. communication ability
    C. joint mobility
    D. motor control
    E. all of the above

22. The goals of physical therapy during the early rehabilitation period after a stroke might include

    A. maintaining range of motion and preventing deformity
    B. improving functional mobility
    C. initiating self-care activities
    D. monitoring changes associated with recovery
    E. all of the above

23. Patients who generally do poorly in rehabilitation programs after a stroke demonstrate all of the following EXCEPT

    A. decreased alertness and poor memory
    B. severe neglect or anosognosia
    C. no medical problems
    D. serious language disturbances
    E. inability to learn new tasks or follow simple commands

24. Positioning of the patient is one of the first considerations during early rehabilitation for a neurologically impaired patient.
    Of the following, the position that should be DISCOURAGED is

    A. lateral side flexion of the head and trunk toward the affected side with head rotation toward the unaffected side
    B. lying on the sound side
    C. lying on the affected side
    D. sitting position
    E. lying in the supine position

25. All of the following are true of range of motion exercises and prevention of limb trauma EXCEPT   25._____

    A. full range of motion should be performed in all shoulder motion
    B. during position changes, care must be taken not to pull on the arm or let it hang unsupported
    C. as spasticity emerges, the use of a sling is generally contraindicated
    D. splinting in a functional position may also be considered
    E. none of the above

KEY (CORRECT ANSWERS)

1.	E	11.	A
2.	E	12.	B
3.	E	13.	D
4.	C	14.	E
5.	B	15.	C
6.	E	16.	B
7.	E	17.	B
8.	D	18.	C
9.	E	19.	E
10.	C	20.	D

21.	E
22.	E
23.	C
24.	A
25.	E

TEST 2

DIRECTIONS: Each question or incomplete statement is followed by several suggested answers or completions. Select the one that BEST answers the question or completes the statement. *PRINT THE LETTER OF THE CORRECT ANSWER IN THE SPACE AT THE RIGHT.*

1. All of the following are common *chronic* peripheral vascular diseases EXCEPT

    A. thromboangitis obliterans
    B. arterial thrombosis
    C. diabetic angiopathy
    D. varicose veins
    E. chronic venous insufficiency

1.____

2. All of the following are *acute* peripheral vascular diseases EXCEPT

    A. embolic occlusion
    B. vasospastic disease
    C. venous thrombosis
    D. arteriosclerosis obliterans
    E. arterial thrombosis

2.____

3. The MOST common form of chronic occlusive vascular disease affecting the lower extremities is

    A. arteriosclerosis obliterans
    B. diabetic angiopathy
    C. varicose veins
    D. chronic venous insufficiency
    E. Buerger's disease

3.____

4. Which of the following is TRUE of Buerger's disease?

    A. Occurs in young males
    B. Predominantly in smokers
    C. First manifests in distal aspects of extremities
    D. Second most common form of chronic occlusive arterial disease
    E. All of the above

4.____

5. The MOST commonly encountered form of acute arterial disease is

    A. arterial embolism
    B. arterial thrombus
    C. vasospastic disease
    D. arteriovenous malformation
    E. none of the above

5.____

6. Brownish pigmentation of skin can be a sign of venous involvement, which is USUALLY caused by

    A. iron
    C. oxyhemoglobin
    E. bilirubin

    B. methemoglobin
    D. hemosiderin

6.____

7. Causes of edema include

    A. increased capillary permeability
    B. decreased osmotic pressure of plasma protein
    C. increased pressure in venules and capillaries
    D. obstruction to lymphatic flow
    E. all of the above

8. Which of the following is a test of peripheral venous circulation?

    A. Rubor of dependency
    B. Percussion test
    C. Venous filling time
    D. Claudication time
    E. None of the above

9. All of the following are tests of peripheral arterial circulation EXCEPT

    A. claudication time
    B. rubor of dependency test
    C. air plethysmography
    D. Doppler ultrasound
    E. venous filling time

10. Which of the following are general instructions for patients with peripheral vascular disease and principles of foot care?

    A. Feet should be washed each night with mild soap and water
    B. Wear clean socks every day
    C. Shoes should be loose-fitting and preferably custom-fitted
    D. Do not use tobacco in any form
    E. All of the above

11. A condition caused by compression of the brachial plexus nerve trunks, with or without vascular compromise, is known as

    A. Erbs palsy
    B. thoracic outlet syndrome
    C. Klumpke's palsy
    D. subclavian steel syndrome
    E. none of the above

12. The MAJOR cause of lower extremity amputation is

    A. trauma
    B. peripheral vascular disease
    C. osteogenic sarcoma
    D. Paget's disease of bone
    E. none of the above

13. The major goals of the preprosthetic rehabilitation program include all of the following EXCEPT

    A. reducing post-operative edema and promoting healing of residual limb
    B. preventing contractures and other complications
    C. maintaining, regaining, or increasing strength in the affected and remaining extremities

D. learning proper care of other extremities
E. none of the above

14. All of the following are advantages of post-operative rigid dressing EXCEPT   14.____

    A. limits post-operative edema development in residual limb
    B. allows for earlier ambulation
    C. allows for earlier fitting of the definitive prosthesis
    D. allows for daily wound inspection and dressing change
    E. configured to each individual residual limb

15. Soft dressing is the oldest method of post-surgical management of residual limbs.   15.____
    The major DISADVANTAGE to soft dressing is that it is

    A. relatively inexpensive
    B. lightweight and readily available
    C. relatively poor controller of edema
    D. easily laundered
    E. none of the above

16. The method of muscle stabilization following amputation in which muscle is sutured to   16.____
    fascia is known as

    A. myodesis   B. myofascial closure
    C. myoplasty   D. rhizotomy
    E. tenodesis

17. Surgical attachment of a tendon to a bone is called   17.____

    A. osteotendenostomy   B. tenodesis
    C. osteotendenosis   D. myodesis
    E. none of the above

18. A temporary prosthesis can be fitted as soon as the wound has healed.   18.____
    All of the following are advantages of temporary prosthesis EXCEPT

    A. it allows early bipedal ambulation
    B. some individuals can return to work
    C. it shrinks the residual limb more effectively than the elastic wrap
    D. it can serve as permanent prosthesis
    E. none of the above

19. OPTIMAL functioning of the prosthesis depends on proper care of the   19.____

    A. socks and sheath   B. prosthesis
    C. amputated and intact limbs D. general health of the patient
    E. all of the above

20. Physical therapists do NOT participate in the management of patients with amputation   20.____
    during the _____ stage.

    A. preoperative   B. postoperative-preprosthetic
    C. prosthetic prescription   D. prosthetic training
    E. none of the above

21. Before prescribing a prosthesis, a physical therapist should evaluate

    A. muscle strength in all limbs
    B. condition of skin
    C. sensory function
    D. circulatory status of the amputation and sound limbs
    E. all of the above

22. One of your patients who had an amputation and now has a below knee prosthesis is complaining of excessive knee flexion.
    All of the following would be prosthetic causes of this condition EXCEPT

    A. high shoe heel
    B. insufficient plantar flexion
    C. flexion contracture
    D. stiff heel cushion
    E. socket too far anterior

23. A patient has a below knee prosthesis. Gait analysis shows excessive lateral thrust. The MOST likely prosthetic cause is

    A. foot outset
    B. excessive foot inset
    C. high shoe heel
    D. flexion contracture
    E. stiff heel cushion

24. While evaluating a patient with an above knee prosthesis, a physiotherapist who was viewing the gait from behind noticed displacement of the prosthesis exhibited in a swing phase.
    Possible prosthetic causes of this condition include all of the following EXCEPT

    A. long prosthesis
    B. locked knee unit
    C. inadequate suspension
    D. abduction contracture
    E. small socket

25. All of the following are anatomic causes of prosthesis abduction noticed during prosthetic assessment EXCEPT

    A. abduction contracture
    B. laterodistal pain
    C. instability
    D. sharp or high medial wall
    E. weak abductors

KEY (CORRECT ANSWERS)

1.	B	11.	B
2.	D	12.	B
3.	A	13.	E
4.	E	14.	D
5.	A	15.	C
6.	D	16.	B
7.	E	17.	B
8.	B	18.	D
9.	C	19.	E
10.	E	20.	E

21. E
22. C
23. B
24. D
25. D

EXAMINATION SECTION
TEST 1

DIRECTIONS: Each question or incomplete statement is followed by several suggested answers or completions. Select the one that BEST answers the question or completes the statement. *PRINT THE LETTER OF THE CORRECT ANSWER IN THE SPACE AT THE RIGHT.*

1. All of the following are guidelines to follow when planning patient and family education EXCEPT:

    A. Give accurate, factual information
    B. Give only as much information as the patient or family needs or can assimilate
    C. Provide a forum for open discussion and communication
    D. Predict expected function or future recovery with confidence
    E. Be supportive, sensitive, and maintain a hopeful manner

1.____

2. It is NOT true that rheumatoid arthritis

    A. is more common in women than men
    B. has increased prevalence with increased age
    C. has a high prevalence among whites
    D. has a low prevalence among Native Americans
    E. has an unknown etiology

2.____

3. Signs and symptoms of rheumatoid arthritis include

    A. morning stiffness
    B. arthritis of 3 or more joint areas
    C. subcutaneous nodules
    D. specific radiological changes in affected joints
    E. all of the above

3.____

4. In a patient with rheumatoid arthritis, when the proximal interphalangeal joint hyperextends and the distal inter-phalangeal joint flexes, it is known as

    A. zigzag effect   B. boutonniere deformity
    C. swan neck deformity   D. subluxation
    E. Bouchard's nodes

4.____

5. Occasionally, in patients with rheumatoid arthritis, the tendon of the extensor digitorum communis will rupture and the unopposed pull of the flexor digitorum profundis will pull the distal interphalangeal joint into flexion. This is known as

    A. boutonniere's deformity   B. zigzag effect
    C. hallux valgus   D. mallet finger
    E. lag phenomenon

5.____

6. The PRIMARY goal of rehabilitation therapy during the acute stage of rheumatoid arthritis is

    A. increased range of motion
    B. reduced pain and inflammation
    C. increased strength of joints

6.____

47

D. joint stability
E. endurance

7. Assessment of the _____ system has key importance in rehabilitation therapy assessment in a patient with rheumatoid arthritis.

   A. circulatory
   B. nervous
   C. musculoskeletal
   D. digestive
   E. cardiovascular

7._____

Questions 8-9.

DIRECTIONS: Questions 8 and 9 are to be answered on the basis of the following information.

A 59-year-old man with rheumatoid arthritis and hallux valgus shows lateral and posterior weight shift on gait analysis.

8. The MOST likely corresponding physical finding would be

   A. lateral deviation of great toe
   B. swelling of first metatarsophalangeal joint
   C. tenderness of great toe
   D. weakness of great toe abduction
   E. none of the above

8._____

9. What would be the physical therapist's treatment goal for this problem?

   A. Increase toe mobility
   B. Accommodate foot with wide toe box shoe
   C. Increase ankle inversion
   D. Diminish pressure with soft insert
   E. None of the above

9._____

10. The cardinal symptoms of multiple sclerosis, termed as charcot's triad, include

    A. intention tremor
    B. scanning speech
    C. nystagmus
    D. all of the above
    E. none of the above

10._____

11. All of the following are true of multiple sclerosis EXCEPT:

    A. Affects predominantly white population
    B. Cause is unknown
    C. Characterized by demyelinating lesions in nervous system
    D. Increased immunoglobulin M
    E. Oligoclonal bands in CSF

11._____

12. All of the following lab studies are used to assist in the diagnosis of multiple sclerosis EXCEPT

    A. radiologic studies
    B. computed tomography
    C. magnetic resonance imaging

12._____

D. lumbar puncture and CSF studies
E. electrophysiologic testing

13. Multiple sclerosis is a chronic, multiple organ system disease. Long-term physical therapy goals for a patient with multiple sclerosis would include

    A. improving functional status and maximizing independence
    B. preventing or retarding development of secondary impairments
    C. promoting emotional, psychological, and social adjustment of patient and family
    D. educating patient and family to maximize retention of rehabilitation gains
    E. all of the above

13.____

14. While providing rehabilitation therapy to a patient with multiple sclerosis, which of the following should be included while assisting with psychological adjustment of patient and family?

    A. Promote understanding of the disease, its symptoms, and management
    B. Emphasize realistic expectations while maintaining hope
    C. Focus on remaining abilities
    D. Educate patient about support group and multiple sclerosis society
    E. All of the above

14.____

15. Of the following, the drug used to treat spasticity in patients with multiple sclerosis is

    A. isoniazid   B. ditropan   C. bactofen
    D. tegretol   E. danazol

15.____

16. Patients with Parkinson's disease typically exhibit all of the following EXCEPT

    A. rigidity
    B. intention tremor
    C. bradykinesia
    D. impaired postural reflexes
    E. dementia

16.____

17. The MOST common form of Parkinson's disease occurring in middle-aged or elderly persons is _____ Parkinsonism.

    A. infectious   B. toxic
    C. idiopathic   D. atypical
    E. pharmacological

17.____

18. Parkinsonian signs are neurochemical in origin and are caused by a DEFICIENCY of the neurotransmitter

    A. epinephrine   B. norepinephrine
    C. dopamine   D. acetylcholine
    E. histidine

18.____

19. Besides the cardinal signs, patients with Parkinson's disease ALSO show

    A. fatigue   B. gait problems
    C. mask-like face   D. dysphagia
    E. all of the above

19.____

20. All of the following are secondary impairments in patients with Parkinson's disease EXCEPT   20.____

    A. muscle atrophy and weakness
    B. hyphosis
    C. weight loss
    D. rigidity
    E. osteoporosis

21. While dopamine is decreased in patients with Parkinson's disease, _____ is increased.   21.____

    A. serotonin   B. acetylcholine
    C. epinephrine   D. norepinephrine
    E. substance P

22. Which of the following should be included in assessing the need for physical therapy in patients with Parkinson's disease?   22.____

    A. Degree of rigidity in response to passive movement
    B. Limitations imposed on active and automatic movements
    C. Which body segments are most affected
    D. Thorough assessment of balance control
    E. All of the above

23. All of the following are indications to the therapist that a patient with Parkinson's disease is experiencing cardiovascular deconditioning EXCEPT   23.____

    A. excessive fatigue   B. shortness of breath
    C. palpitations   D. normal stress test
    E. exercise intolerance

24. An abnormal and involuntary increase in the speed of walking in an attempt to catch up with the displaced center of mass that results from the patient's leaning is called   24.____

    A. hyperkinesia   B. festination
    C. bradykinesia   D. freezing
    E. on-off phenomenon

25. In a patient with Parkinson's disease, the interval between the presentation of stimulus and the start of the movement is called   25.____

    A. movement time   B. festination
    C. reaction time   D. task completion time
    E. none of the above

Questions 26-30.

DIRECTIONS   In Questions 26 through 30, match the numbered muscle with its lettered origin, listed in the column below.

    A. Lateral epicondyle of the humerus
    B. Medial and anterior surface of the ulna
    C. Tendons of the flexor digitorum profundus
    D. Distal fourth of the anterior surface of the ulna
    E. Medial epicondyle of the humerus

26. Flexor digitorum profundus   26.____
27. Supinator   27.____
28. Palnaris longus   28.____
29. Lumbricales   29.____
30. Pronator quadratus   30.____

KEY (CORRECT ANSWERS)

1. D   16. B
2. D   17. C
3. E   18. C
4. C   19. E
5. D   20. D

6. B   21. B
7. C   22. E
8. A   23. D
9. B   24. B
10. D 25. C

11. D 26. B
12. A 27. A
13. E 28. E
14. E 29. C
15. C 30. D

TEST 2

DIRECTIONS: Each question or incomplete statement is followed by several suggested answers or completions. Select the one that BEST answers the question or completes the statement. *PRINT THE LETTER OF THE CORRECT ANSWER IN THE SPACE AT THE RIGHT.*

1. During the middle and late stages of recovery, a patient is out of bed and involved in a variety of activities and therapies.
   The physical therapy goals during this period typically include

   A. preventing or minimizing secondary complications
   B. compensating for sensory and perceptual loss
   C. improving postural control and balance
   D. encouraging socialization and motivation
   E. all of the above

   1.____

2. Which of the following factors affect or influence the outcome of a traumatic head injury?

   A. Premorbid status
   B. Primary damage
   C. Secondary injury
   D. Severity of damage
   E. All of the above

   2.____

3. Primary damage to the brain may be any or all of the following in a patient with traumatic head injury EXCEPT

   A. local brain damage
   B. polar brain damage
   C. hypoxic ischemic injury
   D. mass effect
   E. diffuse brain injury

   3.____

4. All of the following are secondary injuries or complications of traumatic head injury EXCEPT

   A. increased intracranial pressure
   B. diffuse brain injury
   C. obstructive hydrocephalus
   D. posttraumatic epilepsy
   E. hypoxic ischemic injury

   4.____

5. The rating scale that judges level of consciousness and the severity of injury after head trauma is the

   A. Glasgow coma scale
   B. Rancho Los Amigos level of cognitive function
   C. Rappaport's disability rating scale
   D. Glasgow outcome scale
   E. none of the above

   5.____

6. Which of the following tests is used to classify levels of disability ranging from death to no disability?

   A. Glasgow coma scale
   B. Rappaport's disability rating scale
   C. Glasgow outcome scale

   6.____

D. Level of cognitive functioning
E. None of the above

7. Computed tomography is much more useful than magnetic resonance imaging in identifying

    A. cerebral hematomas
    B. ventricular enlargement
    C. atrophy
    D. non-hemorrhagic lesions
    E. none of the above

8. After a traumatic head injury, some patients remain in a decreased level of consciousness, which is known as

    A. comatose
    B. persistent vegetative state
    C. semi-comatose
    D. delirious
    E. none of the above

9. All of the following are caused by uncal herniation of the brain after a head injury EXCEPT

    A. third nerve paresis
    B. hemiparesis
    C. coma
    D. flaccidity
    E. none of the above

10. A transtentorial herniation of the brain involves the

    A. uncus
    B. hippocampus
    C. pons
    D. occulomoor nerve
    E. cerebellar tonsils

11. In tonsillar herniation of the brain, if cerebellar tonsils are involved, _____ may occur.

    A. coma
    B. neck pain and stiffnes
    C. flaccidity
    D. hemiparesis
    E. third nerve palsy

12. An extravascular blood mass located between the dura and the skull is known as a(n) _____ hematoma.

    A. epidural
    B. subdural
    C. subarachnoid
    D. intracranial
    E. supratentorial

13. Head injury can cause a brain injury that results from contact between the surfaces of the brain and cranium called

    A. diffuse brain injury
    B. mass effect
    C. local brain damage
    D. polar brain damage
    E. hypoxic ischeinic injury

14. Polar brain damage MOST commonly affects the

    A. parietal lobe only
    B. cerebellum
    C. midbrain

D. frontal and temporal lobes
E. frontal lobe only

15. The LARGEST organ of the body, which comprises almost 15 percent of total body weight, is the

   A. liver   B. lungs   C. bones   D. skin   E. brain

16. The classic sunburn is the BEST example of

   A. partial thickness burn
   B. deep partial thickness burn
   C. superficial burn
   D. full thickness burn
   E. normal skin

17. The burn wound consists of three zones. In the zone of coagulation,

   A. minimal cell damage occurs
   B. cells are reversibly damaged
   C. skin death occurs
   D. cells may die without treatment
   E. infections occur

18. All of the following are characteristics of a superficial partial thickness burn EXCEPT

   A. whole epidermis is destroyed
   B. upper layer of dermis is destroyed
   C. wound will be bright red
   D. extensive edema
   E. extremely painful

19. The MOST common sign of superficial partial thickness burn is

   A. hyperemia   B. blisters
   C. blanch   D. necrosis
   E. extensive edema

20. All of the following are physiological and biochemical changes following a burn injury EXCEPT

   A. rapid drop in plasma proteins
   B. immediate decrease in IgG
   C. cardiac output decreased
   D. minute ventilation decreased
   E. cortisol production increased

21. The rehabilitation management of a burned patient begins

   A. 48 hours after admission to burn unit
   B. when the patient is out of burn unit
   C. when the patient goes home
   D. the moment the patient arrives at the hospital
   E. after the healing of all wounds

22. After the initial assessment of the depth of the burns and the total amount of body surface area involved, a physical therapist FIRST needs to assess a patient's

    A. ability to talk
    B. ability to breathe
    C. ability to move
    D. self-esteem
    E. state of hydration

22.____

23. It is difficult to list specific goals due to the varied nature of each burn injury. However, typical long-range rehabilitation goals include

    A. attaining a clean burn wound
    B. minimal or no scar contracture
    C. minimal or no pulmonary complications
    D. good to normal strength
    E. all of the above

23.____

24. Which of the following should be included in physical therapy treatment for a burn patient?

    A. Position and splinting
    B. Active and passive exercise
    C. Resistive exercise
    D. Ambulation and massage
    E. All of the above

24.____

25. Scar management is critical during the following 3-6 months. Pressure has been used successfully to minimize hypertrophic scar formation.
Pressure may exert control over hypertrophic scarring by

    A. thinning the dermis
    B. altering the biochemical structure of scar tissue
    C. decreasing blood flow to the area
    D. reorganizing collagen bundles
    E. all of the above

25.____

Questions 26-30.

DIRECTIONS: In Questions 26 through 30, match the numbered muscle with its lettered origin, listed in the column below.

    A. Lateral epicondyle of the humerus
    B. Medial epicondyle of the humerus
    C. Lower two-thirds of the anterior surface of the humerus
    D. Middle third of the posterior surface of the ulna

26. Extensor digitorum   26.____

27. Extensor policis longus   27.____

28. Flexor carpi radialis 28.____

29. Extensor carpi ulnaris 29.____

30. Brachialis 30.____

KEY (CORRECT ANSWERS)

1.	E	16.	C
2.	E	17.	C
3.	C	18.	D
4.	B	19.	B
5.	A	20.	D
6.	B	21.	D
7.	D	22.	C
8.	B	23.	E
9.	D	24.	E
10.	C	25.	E
11.	B	26.	A
12.	A	27.	D
13.	D	28.	B
14.	D	29.	A
15.	D	30.	C

EXAMINATION SECTION
TEST 1

DIRECTIONS: Each question or incomplete statement is followed by several suggested answers or completions. Select the one that BEST answers the question or completes the statement. *PRINT THE LETTER OF THE CORRECT ANSWER IN THE SPACE AT THE RIGHT.*

1. A fusion operation upon the spine is often undertaken to correct 1.____
    A. pelvimetry   B. paroxysm   C. epiphysistis   D. scoliosis

2. The treatment program for slipped epiphysis is MOST similar to the program for 2.____
    A. torticollis   B. Perthe's disease
    C. polydactylism   D. nephrosis

3. Which one of the following conditions is MOST likely to require special educational placement? Fracture of the 3.____
    A. ulna   B. radius   C. femur   D. scapula

4. Which one of the following persons was well-known for his popular newspaper articles on rehabilitation? 4.____
    A. Fred M. Hechinger   B. Howard A Rusk
    C. William M. Cruickshank   D. Merle E. Frampton

5. For the past 20 years, the leading cause of death in children has been 5.____
    A. rheumatic fever   B. poliomyelitis
    C. cancer   D. heart disease

6. Of the following, which one is the MOST frequent cause of long-term crippling conditions in children? 6.____
    A. Infections   B. Congenital defects
    C. Metabolic disturbances D. Unknown causes

7. Which one of the following statements concerning rheumatic fever and heart disease is CORRECT? 7.____
    A. All children who have rheumatic fever will have heart disease.
    B. Some who have had rheumatic fever will have heart disease.
    C. No children who have had rheumatic fever will have heart disease.
    D. All children with heart disease have had rheumatic fever.

8. Of the following, which orthopedic disability gives rise to special educational placement of the LARGEST number of children? 8.____
    A. Slipped epiphysis   B. Multiple sclerosis
    C. Lordosis   D. Otitis

9. A disease in which the muscles appear to be replaced with fatty tissue is
   A. epiphysitis B. kyphosis
   C. muscular dystrophy D. Still's disease

10. Which one of the following BEST defines "a suffix of nouns denoting a morbid condition of growth"?
    A. oma B. itis C. osis D. omy

11. The formation of an artificial anus in the anterior abdominal wall or loin is known as a(n)
    A. anuria B. achondroplasia
    C. colostomy D. plastogene

12. Carpus, ethmoid, and coccyx are
    A. arteries B. bones C. enzymes D. ligaments

13. Inflammation of the intestinal tract is known as
    A. enteritis B. hepatitis
    C. glomerulonephritis D. rhinitis

14. Which one of the following conditions is CORRECTLY paired with an associated disability often found as a secondary defect?
    A. Cerebral palsy – hearing defect B. Chorea – visual defect
    C. Perthe's Disease – speech defect D. Torticollis – poor coordination

15. In which one of the following pairs is it MOST difficult to arrive at a differential diagnosis?
    A. Encephalitis – meningitis B. Aphasia – brain damage
    C. Poliomyelitis – muscular dystrophy D. Hydrocephalia – microcephalia

16. Abnormal brain wave discharges are MOST characteristic of
    A. diabetes B. epilepsy
    C. herpes D. Hansen's disease

17. Polyarthritis is sometimes used as a synonym for
    A. acute rheumatic fever B. arthrochondritis
    C. multiple sclerosis D. polyneuritis

18. Pfeiffer's disease, glandular fever, and infectious mononucleosis are all
    A. the same disease
    B. non-communicable diseases
    C. characterized by a decrease in abnormal mononuclear cells
    D. the result of an intestinal virus

19. Prolongation of the blood clotting time results from a deficiency of vitamin
    A. B2 B. K C. E D. D

20. Which one of the following is classified as a fissure of the brain?   20.____
    A. Maxillary plexuses   B. Periphlebitis
    C. Visceral cleavage   D. Parieto-occipital

21. Paralysis of corresponding parts on two sides of the body is known as   21.____
    A. diplegia   B. hemiplegia   C. monoplegia   D. hemiparesis

22. Muscular dystrophy is a condition in which   22.____
    A. the cause is known
    B. there is apparently no hereditary transmission
    C. several members of the family are often affected in the same manner
    D. the juvenile type is rarely found in boys

23. Tachycardia is a condition of the _____ system.   23.____
    A. skeletal   B. endocrine   C. circulatory   D. digestive

24. Which one of the following diseases involves the lymph nodes and has a   24.____
    poor prognosis?
    A. Colitis   B. Ileitis
    C. Lordosis   D. Hodgkin's Disease

25. Of the following diseases, the one that is NOT directly attributable to a   25.____
    specific vitamin deficiency is
    A. scurvy   B. beriberi   C. tularemia   D. pellagra

KEY (CORRECT ANSWERS)

1. D	11. C
2. B	12. B
3. C	13. A
4. B	14. A
5. D	15. B
6. B	16. B
7. B	17. A
8. A	18. A
9. C	19. B
10. A	20. D

21. A
22. C
23. C
24. D
25. C

TEST 2

DIRECTIONS: Each question or incomplete statement is followed by several suggested answers or completions. Select the one that BEST answers the question or completes the statement. *PRINT THE LETTER OF THE CORRECT ANSWER IN THE SPACE AT THE RIGHT.*

1. The three bones known as the "hammer, anvil, and stirrup" are found in the human
    A. nose   B. knee   C. ear   D. elbow

    1.____

2. Of the following body functions, the one performed by the white blood cells is
    A. carrying carbon dioxide to the lungs
    B. destroying invading bacteria
    C. carrying food particles to the cells
    D. destroying old red blood corpuscles

    2.____

3. Of the following, the word "dyspnea" is MOST closely associated with
    A. bronchial asthma   B. meningitis
    C. rickets   D. synovitis

    3.____

4. A disease characterized by tonic spasms in the voluntarily moved muscles is
    A. osteomyelitis   B. otomycosis
    C. pleuralgia   D. myotonia congenita

    4.____

5. With which one of the following is the term "aura" MOST commonly associated?
    A. Psycho-motor seizures   B. Petit mal seizures
    C. Grand mal seizures   D. Laryngospasm

    5.____

6. Talipes valgus and talipes varus are terms that refer to
    A. postural foot defects   B. congenital hip malformations
    C. bony protrusions   D. ailments of the bladder

    6.____

7. REHABILITATION LITERATURE is a publication issued by the
    A. United States Office of Vocational Rehabilitation
    B. National Society for Crippled Children and Adults
    C. Council for Exceptional Children
    D. American Educational Research Association

    7.____

8. Which one of the following physicians is MOST closely associated with work on tuberculosis of the spine?
    A. Erb   B. Bell   C. Pott   D. Friedreich

    8.____

9. Which one of the following disabilities is apt to require the MOST special precautionary measures on the part of the parent and teacher?
    A. Fragilitas ossium   B. Syndactylism
    C. Rheumatic fever   D. Arthritis

    9.____

60

10. Bursitis, spondylitis, myositis, and sciatica are diseases which are often included under the more general term
    A. thrombosis   B. rheumatism   C. arthritis   D. myxedema

11. An essential difference between nephritis and nephrosis is that nephritis
    A. is a kidney disease; nephrosis is a disease of the liver
    B. may occur at any age; nephrosis occurs only in adulthood
    C. suggests the presence of an inflammation; nephrosis occurs without signs of inflammation
    D. is relatively rare in frequency of occurrence; nephrosis occurs much more frequently

12. Which one of the following is the MAJOR defense that the body utilizes against disease-carrying germs?
    A. Red blood corpuscles   B. Riboflavin
    C. White corpuscles   D. Lymphotomes

13. Research has demonstrated that the number of epileptic seizures may be decreased through the use of psychotherapy. One may conclude from such studies that
    A. epilepsy does not involve organic brain pathology
    B. epilepsy should not be treated chemically
    C. epilepsy involves an inherent personality deformity or disorder
    D. children may react to recognizable emotional crises with hysterical convulsions

14. The wearing of braces, crutches, or casts would be apt to produce the MOST anxiety among children between the ages of
    A. 4-6   B. 7-9   C. 10-12   D. 13-15

15. According to Strauss, brain-injured retardates
    A. have a good attention span
    B. have a poorer vocabulary than the familial retardate
    C. seem to be attracted to the details of an object rather than the whole
    D. go from one task to the next with little effort

16. The transformation of anxiety into bodily symptoms similar to actual physical illness is USUALLY referred to as
    A. conversion hysteria   B. a tic
    C. a phobia   D. a compulsion

17. The following are four types of reaction of physically handicapped children to various situations:
    1) Hysteria   2) Regression
    3) Aggression   4) Attention seeking
    Which two of these reactions are MOST closely related?
    A. 1 and 4   B. 2 and 4   C. 3 and 4   D. 1 and 2

18. Large print reading materials and large charts are likely to be profitably employed for children with
    A. ataxia
    B. multiple sclerosis
    C. ileitis
    D. hemophilia

    18.____

19. A child who takes a regular dosage of Dilantin is PROBABLY suffering from
    A. hepatitis   B. epilepsy   C. nephrosis   D. hypohidrosis

    19.____

20. Broad spectrum antibiotics are used MAINLY for diseases caused by
    A. parasites
    B. allergens
    C. degenerative factors
    D. bacteria

    20.____

21. The name "Cooley" is MOST closely associated with a form of
    A. anemia
    B. dystrophy
    C. asthma
    D. cerebral palsy

    21.____

22. Chorea is a disease of the _____ system.
    A. digestive   B. respiratory   C. circulatory   D. nervous

    22.____

23. "A short lapse of consciousness and a sudden momentary pause in conversation or movement" is MOST suggestive of
    A. nephrosis
    B. autism
    C. Friedreich's ataxia
    D. petit mal seizure

    23.____

24. Which one of the following diseases USUALLY has a very poor prognosis?
    A. Hodgkin's Disease
    B. Slipped epiphysis
    C. Cerebral palsy
    D. Eczema

    24.____

25. Mononucleosis is an abnormal condition of the
    A. blood   B. liver   C. nerves   D. colon

    25.____

KEY (CORRECT ANSWERS)

1.	C	11.	C
2.	B	12.	C
3.	A	13.	D
4.	D	14.	D
5.	C	15.	C
6.	A	16.	A
7.	B	17.	C
8.	C	18.	A
9.	C	19.	B
10.	C	20.	D

21. A
22. D
23. D
24. A
25. A

TEST 3

DIRECTIONS: Each question or incomplete statement is followed by several suggested answers or completions. Select the one that BEST answers the question or completes the statement. *PRINT THE LETTER OF THE CORRECT ANSWER IN THE SPACE AT THE RIGHT.*

1. Increased thirst, increased urination, loss of weight, and general fatigue are COMMON symptoms of 1.____
   A. arthrogryposis   B. diabetes   C. hepatitis   D. arthritis

2. Dementia praecox is now COMMONLY called _____ reaction. 2.____
   A. schizophrenic   B. depressive   C. manic   D. obsessive

3. Which one of the following is a disease of the ear? 3.____
   A. Ostitis   B. Otitis   C. Omphlitis   D. Ophthalmia

4. Glomerulonephritis is a disease of the 4.____
   A. heart   B. stomach   C. kidney   D. larynx

5. Which one of the following is the disease that would MOST likely impair the ability to ambulate? 5.____
   A. Diabetes
   B. Colitis
   C. Bronchiectasis
   D. Spina bifida

6. The lay term "hunchback" is synonymous with 6.____
   A. kyphosis
   B. scoliosis
   C. torticollis
   D. spondylolisthesis

7. Which one of the following diseases involves a malformation of the heart? 7.____
   A. Hydrocele
   B. Tetralogy of Fallot
   C. Myasthenia gravis
   D. Lordosis

8. Of the following, the disease which would be included under the general classification "orthopedic" is 8.____
   A. lupus erythematosus
   B. lymphedema
   C. Osgood-Schlatter's
   D. opthalmospasm

9. Of the following cardiac classifications, the one the teacher would be LEAST likely to encounter is 9.____
   A. 4A   B. 3C   C. 4E   D. 2C

10. Which one of the following diseases is ALWAYS congenital? 10.____
    A. Cerebral palsy
    B. Osteogenesis imperfecta
    C. Rheumatoid arthritis
    D. Pericarditis

11. Of the following, which condition represents a disturbance of the neuro-muscular system frequently accompanied by perceptual difficulties?   11.____
    A. Perthe's disease   B. Cerebral palsy
    C. Spina bifida   D. Talipes

12. The following symptoms are noted in a group of children: enlargement of the calf muscles, difficulty in raising arms, afflicted shoulder and face muscles, waddling gait. The children are PROBABLY suffering from   12.____
    A. spina bifida   B. polio
    C. muscular dystrophy   D. Perthe's disease

13. Of the following diseases, which one is hereditary?   13.____
    A. Scoliosis   B. Osteomyelitis   C. Hemophilia   D. Chorea

14. In which one of the following diseases is overweight FREQUENTLY a concomitant?   14.____
    A. Pott's disease   B. Epilepsy
    C. Slipped epiphysis   D. Coxa vara

15. Hyperactivity is MOST apt to be observed in children who have   15.____
    A. muscular dystrophy   B. brain damage
    C. ileitis   D. rheumatic fever

16. Three broad categories of physical disabilities – orthopedic, cardiac and chronic – are often used for convenience in classifying children. The group below which BEST fits into the category of "chronic" is   16.____
    A. rheumatic fever, muscular dystrophy, kyphosis
    B. nephrosis, colitis, hepatitis
    C. Friedreich's ataxia, osteomyelitis, torticollis
    D. rickets, chorea, arthogryposis

17. Congenital malformation of the brain is often associated with   17.____
    A. hydrocephaly   B. myelitis
    C. varicella   D. lupus erythematosus

18. The use of an electroencephalogram usually proves MOST valuable in the diagnosis of   18.____
    A. epilepsy   B. osteoma   C. lordosis   D. nephritis

19. Incontinence is MOST often an accompanying symptom of   19.____
    A. spina bifida   B. lordosis
    C. Friedreich's ataxia   D. Hodgkin's disease

20. Which one of the following types of cerebral palsy is characterized by uncontrolled movements, facial contortions, and drooling?   20.____
    A. Ataxia   B. Spasticity   C. Athetosis   D. Rigidity

21. Which one of the following diseases may result in brain damage? 21.____
    A. Poliomyelitis   B. Lymphadenoma
    C. Spondylitis   D. Encephalitis

22. A disease USUALLY characterized by frequent vomiting and cramps is 22.____
    A. colitis   B. bronchitis   C. myocarditis   D. empyemia

23. A lateral curvature of the spine is characteristic of 23.____
    A. scoliosis   B. lordosis   C. hyphosis   D. stenosis

24. Which of the following is one of the GREAT dangers of many forms of anemia? 24.____
    A. Brain deterioration   B. Secondary infection
    C. Mental deficiency   D. Bleeding

25. A cleft of the vertebral column with meningeal protrusion is characteristic of 25.____
    A. Sprengel's deformity   B. scoliosis
    C. coxa vara   D. spina bifida

KEY (CORRECT ANSWERS)

1.	B	11.	B
2.	A	12.	C
3.	B	13.	C
4.	C	14.	C
5.	D	15.	B
6.	A	16.	B
7.	B	17.	A
8.	C	18.	A
9.	A	19.	A
10.	B	20.	C

21. D
22. A
23. A
24. B
25. D

TEST 4

DIRECTIONS: Each question or incomplete statement is followed by several suggested answers or completions. Select the one that BEST answers the question or completes the statement. *PRINT THE LETTER OF THE CORRECT ANSWER IN THE SPACE AT THE RIGHT.*

1. When correctly used, the term "allergen" refers to
   A. a person who is allergic
   B. an antihistamine medication
   C. a substance which produces allergy
   D. the tendency to inherit an allergy

2. Which of the following is congenital?
   A. Meningitis
   B. Gastro-enteritis
   C. Chronic bronchitis
   D. Osteogenesis imperfecta

3. Spasm is a common characteristic of
   A. slipped epiphysis
   B. otitis
   C. muscular dystrophy
   D. asthma

4. Which one of the following involves the degeneration of parts of the brain or spinal chord, or both?
   A. Schizophrenia
   B. Spina bifida
   C. Multiple sclerosis
   D. Pott's disease

5. Of the following, the disability with the BEST prognosis is
   A. Cooley's anemia
   B. encephalitis
   C. hemophilia
   D. slipped epiphysis

6. Infectious mononucleosis is also known as
   A. Hodgkin's disease
   B. glandular fever
   C. chorea
   D. bronchiectasis

7. Which one of the following is non-inflammatory?
   A. Cystitis   B. Nephritis   C. Nephrosis   D. Pyelitis

8. Idiopathic epilepsy may be BEST characterized as a condition which
   A. is of unknown origin
   B. is a result of some trauma
   C. is not amenable to treatment
   D. may be safely ignored

9. Which one of the following conditions is characterized by loss of weight, sleeplessness, irritability, and bulging eyes?
   A. Tuberculosis
   B. Overactive thyroid
   C. Myasthenia gravis
   D. Friedreich's ataxia

10. Cardiac involvement may result from a previous acute, infectious disease. 10.____
    The disease referred to is
    A. streptococcus sore throat   B. measles
    C. uremia   D. enteric fever

11. A type of facial paralysis due to a neuritis of the facial nerve in the Fallopian 11.____
    canal is called
    A. Paget's disease   B. Bell's palsy
    C. endocarditis   D. encephalitis

12. A slipped epiphysis occurs MOST frequently in 12.____
    A. early adolescence   B. late adolescence
    C. pre-adolescence   D. early childhood

13. An electroencephalogram would NOT ordinarily be used in connection with 13.____
    A. epilepsy   B. ataxia   C. pyelitis   D. meningitis

14. Which of the following is characterized by lifeless muscle? 14.____
    A. Pott's disease   B. Flaccid paralysis
    C. Scoliosis   D. Colitis

15. The psychologist's report on a child states that he suffers from aphasia. 15.____
    Aphasia is a(n)
    A. impairment of the ability to use or understand spoken language
    B. disturbance of muscular coordination
    C. neurotic reaction characterized by intense fear
    D. inability consciously to recall events or personal identity

16. Which one of the following is MOST likely to be associated with production 16.____
    of large quantities of mucous?
    A. Kyphosis   B. Bronchiectasis
    C. Lymphodenoma   D. Thyroid deficiency

17. Poor bladder control is MOST frequently associated with 17.____
    A. rheumatic fever   B. hemophilia
    C. club foot   D. torticollis

18. Excessive accumulation of cerebrospinal fluid within the skull is USUALLY 18.____
    characterized as
    A. mongolism   B. microcephaly
    C. macrocephaly   D. hydrocephaly

19. Cerebral palsy is a term applied to a group of conditions having in common 19.____
    A. hereditary malformation   B. retarded mentality
    C. microcephalic appearance   D. disorders of muscular control

20. Which one of the following conditions is caused by the inflammation of the lower part of the intestine? 20.____
    A. Pyelitis
    B. Transverse myelitis
    C. Regional ileitis
    D. Hepatitis

21. In contrast with former treatment methods that called for intramuscular injections, oral medication is now frequently provided for treating 21.____
    A. diabetes   B. colitis   C. thyroiditis   D. myelitis

22. A child who has cerebral palsy has difficulty in keeping his paper on his desk. Which one of the following materials should his teacher provide to help him? 22.____
    A. A thick piece of oaktag
    B. A paperweight
    C. Masking tape
    D. A set of tacks

23. A bone fracture which is in the process of healing will call for GREATER intake of 23.____
    A. vitamin B complex
    B. folic acid
    C. vitamins D and C
    D. vitamins A and K

24. Antihistamines are often used in treating 24.____
    A. allergies
    B. anemias
    C. glandular fevers
    D. adrenal hemorrhages

25. An underweight child with a cardiac condition should be encouraged to 25.____
    A. add candy to his diet
    B. add carbohydrates such as bread and milk desserts to his diet
    C. maintain weight below normal since this ensures a margin of safety should illness occur
    D. increase his intake of fluids and salt

KEY (CORRECT ANSWERS)

1. C
2. D
3. D
4. C
5. D

6. B
7. C
8. A
9. B
10. A

11. B
12. A
13. C
14. B
15. A

16. C
17. A
18. D
19. D
20. C

21. A
22. C
23. C
24. A
25. B

TEST 5

DIRECTIONS: Each question or incomplete statement is followed by several suggested answers or completions. Select the one that BEST answers the question or completes the statement. *PRINT THE LETTER OF THE CORRECT ANSWER IN THE SPACE AT THE RIGHT.*

1. Which of the following diseases has yielded to chemotherapeutic treatment in recent years?
    A. Multiple sclerosis
    B. Tuberculosis
    C. Diabetes
    D. Scleroderma

2. The MOST satisfactory results in the treatment of epilepsy have been obtained through the use of
    A. vitamins
    B. diet
    C. drugs
    D. exercise

3. A physically handicapped child is enclosed in a box which enables her to stand and work. The child PROBABLY suffers from
    A. scoliosis
    B. Perthe's disease
    C. spina bifida
    D. cerebral palsy

4. In which of the following are the contributing authorities CORRECTLY matched with the area of work indicated?
    A. Epilepsy – Lennox, Putnam
    B. Cardiovascular diseases – White, Cruickshank
    C. Rehabilitation – Salk, Deaver
    D. Cerebral palsy – Phelps, De La Chappelle

5. Sound vibrations are transmitted to the brain by the
    A. nerves in the inner ear
    B. nerves in the middle ear
    C. ear drum
    D. nerves of the outer ear

6. Of the following, which disease requires STRICTEST control of the time interval between meals?
    A. Rheumatic fever
    B. Allergy
    C. Diabetes
    D. Epilepsy

7. Of the following, which disease is MUCH MORE prevalent now than it was twenty years ago?
    A. Poliomyelitis
    B. Spina bifida
    C. Hemophilia
    D. Infectious hepatitis

8. Which one of the following approaches to the treatment of epilepsy has been MOST successful in recent years?
    A. Drug therapy
    B. Special diets
    C. Psychotherapy
    D. Shock therapy

9. Early research in the education of brain-injured children without motor handicaps was done by
   A. Cruickshank   B. Barker   C. Lehtinen   D. Fouracre

10. In recent years, particular attention has been paid to the educational problems presented by
    A. the brain injured
    B. hemophiliacs
    C. the orthopedically handicapped
    D. children with muscular dystrophy

11. Which one of the following may result in brain damage and mental deficiency?
    A. Meningitis and encephalitis
    B. Poliomyelitis and chorea
    C. Scarlet fever and enuresis
    D. Rheumatic fever and arthritis

12. The exact cause of rheumatic fever is unknown, but in susceptible individuals an attack is frequently proceded by
    A. respiratory streptococcal infection
    B. recurrent migraine disturbance
    C. a violent spasm of intestinal distress
    D. sustained and intense feverish disorder

13. The MOST frequent glandular condition associated with mental retardation is a deficiency in the functioning of the _____ gland.
    A. pineal   B. thyroid   C. pituitary   D. adrenal

14. Some authorities maintain that the inability of the body to utilize a vitamin properly is a causative factor in
    A. epilepsy
    B. muscular dystrophy
    C. chorea
    D. achondroplasia

15. Glandular fever is sometimes referred to as
    A. mononucleosis
    B. myasthenia gravis
    C. monoplegia
    D. ileitis

16. A metabolic disease in which there is persistent hyperglycaemia, excessive thirst, and loss of weight is
    A. cancer
    B. heart disease
    C. diabetes
    D. Addison's disease

17. Insulin, which enables the body to utilize and store sugar properly, is produced by the
    A. liver
    B. Islands of Langerhans
    C. spleen
    D. bone marrow

18. Victims of rheumatic fever are prone to develop chronic forms of
    A. dyspepsia and dysphagia
    B. sore throats and tonsillitis
    C. migraine and asthma
    D. intestinal and muscular disorder

19. A child with a positive EEG reading is likely to have
    A. asthma
    B. rheumatic fever
    C. convulsive disorders
    D. nephritis

20. Spasticity may reduce a child's ability to respond accurately to a teacher's questions requiring
    A. use of the sense of touch
    B. recall of prior learning
    C. knowledge of subject matter
    D. familiarity with domestic routines

21. Of the following, which child is MOST apt to encounter difficulty in handling spatial relationships? The child with
    A. spina bifida
    B. ulcerative colitis
    C. Pott's disease
    D. cerebral palsy

22. Which one of the following is characterized by involuntary, abnormal movements in the extremities?
    A. Myositis
    B. Rheumatic fever
    C. Athetosis
    D. Scoliosis

23. Of the following, the disease that is believed to have strong psychosomatic implications is
    A. colitis   B. diabetes   C. anemia   D. hepatitis

24. Which one of the following is a congenital disease that involves the internal organs of the body?
    A. Cystic fibrosis
    B. Nephritis
    C. Tuberculosis
    D. Synovitis

25. Of the following disabilities, the one MOST likely to require a body cast is
    A. muscular dystrophy
    B. scoliosis
    C. esophagitis
    D. torticollis

KEY (CORRECT ANSWERS)

1.	B	11.	A
2.	C	12.	A
3.	D	13.	B
4.	A	14.	B
5.	A	15.	A
6.	C	16.	C
7.	D	17.	B
8.	A	18.	B
9.	C	19.	C
10.	A	20.	A

21. D
22. C
23. A
24. A
25. B

TEST 6

DIRECTIONS: Each question or incomplete statement is followed by several suggested answers or completions. Select the one that BEST answers the question or completes the statement. *PRINT THE LETTER OF THE CORRECT ANSWER IN THE SPACE AT THE RIGHT.*

1. Arteriosclerosis is a disturbance of the _____ system.   1.____
   A. skeletal   B. endocrine   C. nervous   D. circulatory

2. Of the following disorders, which one is NOT a form of cerebral palsy?   2.____
   A. Little's disease   B. Athetosis
   C. Mitral stenosis   D. Spastic paralysis

3. The chin is rotated away from the side of the short, prominent muscle; the head is tilted toward the affected side. These symptoms are characteristic of   3.____
   A. talipes   B. torticollis   C. ligamentitis   D. bursitis

4. A patient designated by a physician as "Class IID" is suffering from   4.____
   A. diabetes   B. polio
   C. tuberculosis   D. heart disease

5. A dorsal curvature is GENERALLY referred to as   5.____
   A. lordosis   B. hyphosis   C. scoliosis   D. curatosis

6. A disease that usually occurs in overweight boys and girls between the ages of ten and thirteen years, and is characterized by upper tibial epiphysitis is known as _____ disease.   6.____
   A. Pott's   B. Charcot-Tooth's
   C. Little's   D. Osgood-Schlatter's

7. A child whose walk is characterized by a scissors gait, with inward rotation and adduction of the legs, is PROBABLY suffering from   7.____
   A. Erb's palsy   B. spasticity
   C. osteogenesis imperfecta   D. spina bifida

8. Which one of the following groups encompasses the LARGEST number of children?   8.____
   A. Malnourished   B. Crippled   C. Cardiac   D. Tuberculosis

9. Rickets, a disease of nutrition manifested by disturbance in the general health and in the bones and joints, is caused by a lack of vitamin   9.____
   A. A   B. B   C. C   D. D

10. Rheumatic fever   10.____
    A. most often strikes children between the ages of 9 and 10
    B. is generally thought to be a streptococcal infection
    C. is generally accompanied by pain in the region of the heart
    D. is contagious

75

11. A young girl has to have a blood transfusion every two weeks. She PROBABLY is suffering from
    A. gastritis
    B. hepatitis
    C. nephritis
    D. Cooley's disease

12. Differential diagnosis is MOST difficult in distinguishing between cases of
    A. poliomyelitis and meningitis
    B. aphasia and brain damage
    C. spasticity and athetosis
    D. leukemia and anemia

13. In using the Snellen letter chart, an "eye test line" should be marked on the floor in the classroom _____ from the chart.
    A. 15'
    B. 20'
    C. 25'
    D. 30'

14. Adults normally have _____ teeth.
    A. 40
    B. 36
    C. 32
    D. 28

15. Of the following, the MOST important function of the sweat glands is to
    A. remove salt from the blood
    B. cool the body through evaporation
    C. cleanse the pores in the skin
    D. reduce body weight

16. Which of the following is CORRECTLY matched with the vitamin or mineral that counteracts it?
    A. Eye ailments – Vitamin K
    B. Anemia – Vitamin A
    C. Failure in blood clotting – Iron
    D. Goiter – Iodine

17. A well-balanced diet should include foods rich in minerals because they furnish the body with
    A. materials for the repair of body tissues
    B. materials for building strong teeth and bones
    C. materials for growing nails and hair
    D. energy for work

18. A physical handicap is MOST likely to be a disturbing influence to the child who is
    A. between the ages of 3 and 8
    B. between the ages of 8 and 12
    C. an adolescent
    D. a post-adolescent

19. A young aphasic child
    A. always understands what is said to him but cannot respond vocally
    B. always has a hearing loss in addition to his language disorder
    C. is usually mentally retarded
    D. shows many of the same characteristics and symptoms associated with deafness

20. The proportion of children with cerebral palsy who have IQ's below 70 is APPROXIMATELY
    A. 30%
    B. 50%
    C. 70%
    D. 90%

21. Considerable progress has been made in the outpatient treatment of the emotionally disturbed individual through the use of
    A. prefrontal lobotomy
    B. chemotherapy
    C. shock treatment
    D. hydrotherapy

21.____

22. Personality studies of physically handicapped persons and persons not so handicapped show that
    A. there is no significant difference in frequency of personality problems between the two groups
    B. the most frequent personality deviation of the physically handicapped person is withdrawing behavior
    C. persons with closely similar disabilities tend to develop similar personality structures
    D. nearly all physically handicapped persons exhibit evidence of personality difficulties

22.____

23. The MOST common reaction of the physically handicapped child to separation from the family because of hospitalization is
    A. depression   B. projection   C. regression   D. sublimation

23.____

24. Psychologists generally agree that, when an emotional handicap exists in a person who has a physical disability, the emotional handicap
    A. usually stems directly from the physical handicap
    B. is usually much the same in all persons with that particular physical disability
    C. does not stem directly from the disability, but has been mediated by social variables
    D. is apt to be extremely severe

24.____

25. The ability of physically handicapped individuals to cope satisfactorily with ridicule and other difficult situations
    A. depends largely on the attitudes of society toward the handicapped
    B. may be strengthened by special training in social techniques
    C. decreases as the handicapped individual matures
    D. is a function of the sex of the individual

25.____

KEY (CORRECT ANSWERS)

1. D
2. C
3. B
4. D
5. B

6. D
7. B
8. A
9. D
10. B

11. D
12. B
13. B
14. C
15. B

16. D
17. B
18. C
19. D
20. B

21. B
22. B
23. C
24. C
25. B

EXAMINATION SECTION
TEST 1

DIRECTIONS: Each question or incomplete statement is followed by several suggested answers or completions. Select the one that BEST answers the question or completes the statement. *PRINT THE LETTER OF THE CORRECT ANSWER IN THE SPACE AT THE RIGHT.*

1. Studies show that handicapped persons rehabilitated under the state-federal vocational rehabilitation program repay in Federal income taxes *alone* the Federal government's ENTIRE investment in their rehabilitation within _____ year(s).

    A. one   B. three   C. six   D. ten

2. It is estimated that the number of individuals added to those who need vocational rehabilitation services each year in the United States approximates

    A. 50,000   B. 250,000   C. 1,000,000   D. 25,000,000

3. National *Employ the Physically Handicapped Week* is USUALLY observed during the month of

    A. February   B. May   C. August   D. October

4. The one of the following of the Federal aid programs of public assistance which was MOST recently developed is aid to

    A. citizens over 65 years of age not covered by social security
    B. dependent children
    C. permanently and totally disabled individuals
    D. the blind

5. The one of the following providing placement services for the physically handicapped which restricts its activities to veterans is

    A. Federation Employment Service
    B. Fifty-two Association
    C. Just-One-Break Committee
    D. Vocational Advisory Service

6. The one of the following hospitals which does NOT have a full physical medicine and rehabilitation service with a complete rehabilitation *team* is

    A. Bellevue   B. Bird S. Coler
    C. Goldwater Memorial   D. James Ewing

7. Of the following programs of services to the physically handicapped, the one which is a division of the State Department of Education is

    A. Governor's Committee on Employment of the Physically Handicapped
    B. State Rehabilitation Hospital
    C. Vocational Rehabilitation
    D. Workmen's Compensation

8. The one of the following which constitutes the LARGEST professional group in the National Rehabilitation Association is

   A. counselors
   B. occupational therapists
   C. physical therapists
   D. physicians

9. Three of the following conduct vocational training services for the handicapped. The one which does NOT is

   A. Altro Workshops
   B. American Rehabilitation Committee
   C. The Institute of Physical Medicine and Rehabilitation
   D. The Lighthouse

10. The one of the following that has a sheltered workshop IN ADDITION TO its other rehabilitation facilities is

    A. Bellevue Hospital Physical Medicine and Rehabilitation Service
    B. Hospital for Special Surgery
    C. Institute of Physical Medicine and Rehabilitation
    D. Institute for the Crippled and Disabled

11. The one of the following agencies that does NOT provide direct services to the handicapped is the

    A. American Rehabilitation Committee
    B. Federation of the Handicapped
    C. Goodwill Rehabilitation Committee
    D. International Society for the Welfare of Cripples

12. Of the following agencies, the one which is PARTICULARLY known for its program of rehabilitation for the tuberculous is the

    A. Altro Workshops
    B. Brooklyn Bureau of Social Service
    C. Federation of the Handicapped
    D. Goodwill Industries

13. Of the following agencies, the one which does NOT provide vocational counseling services for the physically handicapped is the

    A. Bureau of Social Services
    B. Federation Employment Service
    C. Fountain House
    D. Just-One-Break Committee

14. The one of the following publications which would be LEAST likely to be of professional interest to a rehabilitation counselor is

    A. COMEBACK
    B. JOURNAL OF REHABILITATION
    C. JOURNAL OF THE ASSOCIATION FOR PHYSICAL AND MENTAL REHABILITATION
    D. PERFORMANCE

15. Each municipal hospital which has a department of physical medicine and rehabilitation has a *rehabilitation team.*
    The one of the following occupations which is NOT represented on that team is

    A. bracemaker
    B. physiatrist
    C. psychologist
    D. recreation leader

16. Of the following, the one which is NOT considered to be a medical center is

    A. Beekman-Downtown
    B. Columbia-Presbyterian
    C. New York-Cornell
    D. New York University-Bellevue

17. The National Institutes of Health are a part of the

    A. Kellogg Foundation
    B. National Research Council
    C. Rockefeller Foundation
    D. U.S. Public Health Service

18. Results of I.Q. tests are used as predictors of all of the following EXCEPT

    A. learning disabilities
    B. educational achievement
    C. job performance
    D. athletic ability

19. The index usually used to describe an individual's relative mental brightness is

    A. C.A.   B. E.Q.   C. I.Q.   D. M.A.

20. Of the following, the BEST criterion of an individual's normalcy is his

    A. educational goals
    B. interpersonal relationships
    C. moral values
    D. physical standards

21. The one of the following which has been greatly expanded by federal legislation is the

    A. counseling services for disabled veterans provided by the Veterans Administration
    B. federal-state vocational rehabilitation program
    C. rehabilitation training activities of the Children's Bureau
    D. selective placement activities of the various state employment services

22. The one of the following who would be LEAST likely to qualify for services under the federal-state vocational rehabilitation program is a

    A. college student paralyzed by poliomyelitis
    B. migratory worker stricken by multiple sclerosis
    C. self-employed man, fifty years of age, disabled by arthritis
    D. worker suffering from an amputation as a result of an industrial accident

23. Of the following, the present policy governing provision of medical services by the Veterans Administration to veterans with non-service connected disabilities is that

    A. if a veteran cannot afford to pay for medical care, and if a bed is available, he can receive in-patient care
    B. if a veteran cannot afford to pay for medical care, he can receive out-patient care
    C. in-patient care can be given only to those with tuberculosis
    D. out-patient care can be given only to those with psychiatric problems

24. In terms of vocational rehabilitation, the MOST important area of information which the counselor must know about the patient is his

    A. educational achievement
    B. expressed goal
    C. previous job experience
    D. type of military service discharge

25. The type of counseling MOST likely to benefit a patient who is still unable to accept his disability two years after injury has occurred is

    A. educational B. personal C. social D. vocational

KEY (CORRECT ANSWERS)

1.	B		11.	D
2.	B		12.	A
3.	D		13.	C
4.	C		14.	C
5.	B		15.	A
6.	D		16.	A
7.	C		17.	D
8.	A		18.	D
9.	C		19.	C
10.	D		20.	B

21. B
22. B
23. A
24. B
25. B

TEST 2

DIRECTIONS: Each question or incomplete statement is followed by several suggested answers or completions. Select the one that BEST answers the question or completes the statement. *PRINT THE LETTER OF THE CORRECT ANSWER IN THE SPACE AT THE RIGHT.*

1. The development of objective criteria for measuring the physical capacities of patients is MOST difficult in cases of   1.____

    A. coronary heart disease B. multiple sclerosis
    C. poliomyelitis D. rheumatoid arthritis

2. The prognosis for vocational rehabilitation is LEAST favorable in cases of   2.____

    A. amputation of both upper extremities
    B. diabetes
    C. hemiplegia
    D. muscular dystrophy

3. The term used for a medical specialist in *physical medicine and rehabilitation* is   3.____

    A. orthopedist B. physiatrist
    C. physical therapist D. physiotherapist

4. It is *generally* accepted that the sense through which people learn MOST readily is the   4.____

    A. auditory B. kinesthetic C. tactile D. visual

5. An obturator is FREQUENTLY used with persons afflicted with   5.____

    A. aphasia B. cleft palate
    C. lisping D. stuttering

6. Visual acuity of *20/200 or less* is USUALLY interpreted as   6.____

    A. ability to discriminate between light and dark
    B. complete blindness
    C. remediable with glasses
    D. industrial blindness

7. Of the following, the BEST means for testing hearing ability is the   7.____

    A. audiometer
    B. hearing aid
    C. medical examination of the ear
    D. watch tick test

8. Recent studies indicate that adults suffering from a hearing loss, when compared to those with normal hearing, are *usually* MORE   8.____

    A. aggressive B. intelligent C. shy D. stable

9. The perception of one's own muscular movement is called   9.____

    A. cataplasia B. kinesthesia
    C. synesthesia D. none of the above

10. The one of the following types of speech disorders which will *usually* respond to therapy and retraining in the SHORTEST time is

    A. articulatory disorders
    B. cleft palate speech
    C. post-laryngectomy speech
    D. stuttering

11. As a result of medical care advances, there has been, within recent years, a lessening of the need for rehabilitation counseling services in hospitals for patients with

    A. amputations
    B. arthritis
    C. hemiplegia
    D. tuberculosis

12. The one of the following conditions which is NOT characterized by an orthopedic involvement is

    A. amputations
    B. congenital club foot
    C. diabetes
    D. scoliosis

13. The use of isonicotinic hydrazides in connection with other forms of therapy is a RECENT development in the treatment of

    A. arthritis
    B. cerebral palsy
    C. muscular dystrophy
    D. tuberculosis

14. The one of the following diseases in which insulin is used as a method of medical control and management is

    A. diabetes
    B. epilepsy
    C. rheumatic fever
    D. syphilis

15. The one of the following with which aphasia is MOST commonly associated is

    A. hemiplegia   B. monoplegia   C. paraplegia   D. quadraplegia

16. The kind of patient with which a rehabilitation counselor in a municipal hospital would come into professional contact LEAST frequently is the

    A. geriatric   B. neurologic   C. orthopedic   D. psychiatric

17. In the development of the embryo, the month after which the central nervous system, origin of overt human behavior, is well under way is the

    A. second   B. fifth   C. seventh   D. ninth

18. Three of the following symptoms are frequently associated with multiple sclerosis. The one which is NOT is

    A. metabolic disturbances
    B. speech difficulties
    C. stumbling gait
    D. visual disturbances

19. Of the following, the term which does NOT describe a type of cerebral palsy is

    A. amebiasis   B. ataxic   C. athetoid   D. spastic

20. Three of the following diseases are frequently progressive in the chronic stages. The one which is NOT is

    A. multiple sclerosis
    B. muscular dystrophy
    C. Parkinson's disease
    D. poliomyelitis

21. Three of the following are diseases usually classified as chronic neurological diseases. The one which does NOT fall into this category is

    A. cerebral palsy
    B. multiple sclerosis
    C. muscular dystrophy
    D. rheumatism

22. The one of the following books that should be of MOST interest to the cerebral palsied is

    A. BORN THAT WAY by Earl R. Carlson
    B. IT WAS NOT MY OWN IDEA by Robinson Pierce
    C. TRIUMPH CLEAR by Lorraine L. Beim
    D. WHO WALK ALONE by Perry Burgess

23. In general, the percentage of patients stricken with poliomyelitis who will be severely disabled is *approximately*

    A. 20%   B. 45%   C. 75%   D. 90%

24. With the development of anticonvulsant drugs, the percentage of persons with epilepsy whose seizures can now be completely controlled is *approximately*

    A. 10%   B. 33%   C. 50%   D. 75%

25. The one of the following diseases which affects the SMALLEST number of persons is

    A. arteriosclerosis
    B. congenital heart disease
    C. hypertension
    D. rheumatic fever

26. Recent advances in the research and treatment of epilepsy have resulted from the development and widespread use of the

    A. electrocardiograph
    B. electroencephalograph
    C. electromyograph
    D. electronic microscope

27. The one of the following books that should be MOST interesting to parents of a congenital amputee is

    A. AND NOW TO LIVE AGAIN by Betsy Barton
    B. OUT ON A LIMB by Louise Baker
    C. THE CHILD WHO NEVER GREW by Pearl Buck
    D. TRIUMPH OF LOVE by Leona Bruckner

28. The one of the following responsible for the GREATEST number of patients in mental hospitals is

    A. drug addiction
    B. paresis
    C. schizophrenia
    D. senile dementia

29. Of the following, the LEAST important factor in counseling a patient with a unilateral BK amputation is

    A. diagnosis
    B. etiology
    C. site of amputation
    D. type of prosthetic device worn

30. One of the MOST comprehensive references on the psychological aspects of the physically disabled is that compiled by 30.____

    A. Bitner   B. Garrett   C. Kessler   D. Zohl

KEY (CORRECT ANSWERS)

1.	A	16.	D
2.	D	17.	A
3.	B	18.	A
4.	D	19.	A
5.	B	20.	D
6.	D	21.	D
7.	A	22.	A
8.	C	23.	A
9.	B	24.	C
10.	A	25.	B
11.	D	26.	B
12.	C	27.	D
13.	D	28.	C
14.	A	29.	D
15.	A	30.	B

EXAMINATION SECTION
TEST 1

DIRECTIONS: Each question or incomplete statement is followed by several suggested answers or completions. Select the one that BEST answers the question or completes the statement. *PRINT THE LETTER OF THE CORRECT ANSWER IN THE SPACE AT THE RIGHT.*

1. All of the following are associated with movement of the femur at the hip joint EXCEPT: 1.____

    A. Flexion - outward rotation
    B. Inversion - supination
    C. Inward rotation - circumduction
    D. Extension - abduction

2. Of the following, the one necessary for the formation of thyroxin, which controls the metabolic rate, is 2.____

    A. phosphorus   B. sodium chloride
    C. iodine   D. calcium

3. Excluding the coronary circulation, the average time for the complete circulation of the blood through all the circuits of the adult human body is APPROXIMATELY 3.____

    A. 23 seconds   B. 5 minutes
    C. 1 minute, 15 seconds D. 10 minutes

4. Of the following, the substance necessary for the clotting of blood is 4.____

    A. ptyalin   B. prothrombin
    C. gastrin   D. rennin

5. Of the following, the ones which CANNOT be converted into heat or other forms of energy are 5.____

    A. fats   B. proteins
    C. minerals   D. carbohydrates

6. Of the following suggestions for reducing weight, the one MOST likely to be given by doctors to their otherwise healthy patients is to 6.____

    A. omit all desserts and bread
    B. increase the protein intake, to omit duplication in starches at each meal, and to eat low calorie desserts
    C. omit potatoes, bread, and all desserts except fruit for the main meal
    D. follow a diet made up entirely of protein, fruit, and vegetables

7. Blood sugar is low 7.____

    A. in untreated diabetes mellitus
    B. during emotional stress
    C. after meals
    D. during severe and prolonged muscular exertion

8. The substances which are NOT necessary for building new tissues are 8.____

    A. water   B. carbohydrates
    C. proteins   D. minerals

9. A nutrient functions in any or all of the following ways EXCEPT to

   A. furnish energy
   B. provide materials for building or maintenance of body tissues
   C. help regulate body processes
   D. purify the blood

10. It is most important to see that reducing diets of adolescents do NOT lack

    A. fats
    B. proteins
    C. carbohydrates
    D. simple sugars

11. The CHIEF value of cellulose in the diet is that it

    A. is more soluble than starch
    B. gives bulk to the intestinal residues
    C. is easily digested
    D. provides an essential amino acid

12. It is CORRECT to state that enzymes

    A. are used up in chemical reactions of foods
    B. retard the process of breaking down of foods
    C. work only in acid surroundings
    D. are specific in their action

13. The acetabulum is the articular cup in a bone which acts as a socket for the

    A. clavicle   B. femur   C. radius   D. tibia

14. Of the following associations, the CORRECT one is:

    A. Second class lever - the forearm when it is being extended by the triceps muscle
    B. Third class lever - the foot, when rising on the toes
    C. First class lever - the head, tipping forward and backward
    D. Second class lever - the arm when it is raised sideward-upward by the deltoid muscle

15. All of the following are correct principles relating to the muscular system EXCEPT:

    A. Muscles contract more rapidly following warm-up activities
    B. Muscular strength is progressively developed by the repetition of exercises of the same intensity
    C. Muscles contract more forcefully if they are first stretched, provided that they are not overstretched
    D. A muscle must be loaded beyond its customary load if strength is to be increased

16. Gradations in muscular contraction are related to

    A. variations in intensity of muscular contraction
    B. the number of fibers in the muscle which contract
    C. the circulation of blood within the muscle
    D. the manufacture of lactic acid in the muscle

17. In order to determine the basal metabolic rate of an individual, all of the following conditions must be included EXCEPT that the

    A. environment temperature must be comfortably warm
    B. test must be made from 12 to 18 hours after the last meal
    C. body must be in the waking state and at complete rest
    D. test should be preceded by a ten-minute period of vigorous exercise

18. The center of gravity of an individual of average build in an erect standing position is

    A. located in the pelvis in front of the upper part of the sacrum
    B. located at the articulation of the femur and the pelvis
    C. located in the anterior wall of the pelvis
    D. lower in men than in women because of anatomical structure

19. All of the following statements concerning lateral curvatures of the spine are correct EXCEPT:

    A. Some rotation of the vertebrae always accompanies lateral flexion of the spine
    B. In a simple structural lateral curvature, the curve is confined to one region and there is no compensatory curve
    C. The shoulder on the side of a dorsal convexity is lower than the other shoulder
    D. In a functional lateral curvature of the spine, the curve disappears when the individual suspends his body by hanging from the arms

20. When taking the wrist pulse rate, one should AVOID

    A. taking the pulse with the thumb
    B. counting the pulse beats for 1 minute, then checking the rate by counting for another minute
    C. having the patient support his arm and hand in a relaxed position
    D. taking the pulse on the thumb side of the wrist between the tendon and the wrist bone

21. Ringworm is caused by a microscopic

    A. mold B. worm C. yeast D. virus

22. All of the following associations of suffixes found in technical terms on a health record and meanings are correct EXCEPT:

    A. Osis - swelling
    B. Emia - blood
    C. Itis - inflammation
    D. Algia - pain

23. All of the following statements are correct EXCEPT:

    A. The presence of a sufficient quantity of fats in the diet does away with the necessity of using protein for fuel.
    B. Any considerable amount of fat in food eaten will slow down the digestion of the whole meal.
    C. The digestion of fats begins in the stomach.
    D. Layers of fat under the skin help to keep the body temperature constant.

4 (#1)

24. The body's CHIEF means of increasing heat production is by   24._____
    A. perspiring
    B. dilating the blood vessels
    C. shivering
    D. none of the above

25. All of the following concerning the feet are correct EXCEPT: 25._____
    A. The height of the arch is an indication of the strength of the foot
    B. Arch supports are temporary expedients for the relief of foot pain
    C. Neglected, weak feet become flexible, flat feet
    D. Rigid flat feet show depressed arches when the weight is not borne on the feet

KEY (CORRECT ANSWERS)

1. B		11. B	
2. C		12. D	
3. A		13. B	
4. B		14. C	
5. C		15. B	
6. B		16. B	
7. D		17. D	
8. B		18. A	
9. D		19. C	
10. B		20. A	

21. A
22. A
23. C
24. C
25. A

TEST 2

DIRECTIONS: Each question or incomplete statement is followed by several suggested answers or completions. Select the one that BEST answers the question or completes the statement. *PRINT THE LETTER OF THE CORRECT ANSWER IN THE SPACE AT THE RIGHT.*

1. The INCORRECT association is: 1.____

    A. Endomorph - soft, round, tendency to lay on fat
    B. Somatomorph - tall, athletic, broad-shouldered
    C. Ectomorph - linear, fragile, delicate
    D. Mesomorph - square, rugged, hard

2. All of the following statements concerning protein are correct EXCEPT: 2.____

    A. Protein is a source of energy
    B. Protein is required for tissue building and repair
    C. Vegetable proteins are generally as satisfactory as meat proteins in meeting body requirements
    D. Cheese contains important animal proteins

3. Foods rich in calcium and protein are also the BEST sources of 3.____

    A. iodine
    B. phosphorus
    C. copper
    D. fluorine

4. With regard to nutrition, the CORRECT statement is: 4.____

    A. Malnutrition is found only in low-income families
    B. Obesity is generally due to faulty glands
    C. Nutrition is affected by rest, recreation, and general mental health
    D. Adolescents should take additional vitamin preparations in order to insure adequate vitamin intake

5. In order to improve the muscular state of the nation, it would be desirable to do all of the following for our youth EXCEPT to 5.____

    A. encourage participation in daily calisthenics
    B. promote participation in swimming
    C. popularize soccer as a game for school children
    D. emphasize competitive sports

6. The grating of the broken pieces of a bone in a simple fracture is called 6.____

    A. crepitus
    B. contusion
    C. chorisis
    D. comminution

7. All of the following associations of pressure points and bleeding points are correct EXCEPT: 7.____

    A. Brachial artery - bleeding from the wrist
    B. Carotid artery - bleeding from the shoulder joint
    C. Subclavian artery - bleeding from the arm
    D. Femoral artery - bleeding from the lower leg

8. Of the following associations of fractures and distinguishing characteristics, the CORRECT one is

   A. Colles' fracture - radial bone
   B. compound fracture - point of fracture in contact with the external surface of the body
   C. Pott's fracture - tibiofibular joint
   D. Greenstick fracture - broken ends of the bone are interlocked

9. Foods which provide for growth and body repair must be rich in

   A. carbohydrates
   B. fats
   C. minerals
   D. proteins

10. Of the following, the one which is the BEST source of iron is

    A. milk
    B. liver
    C. prunes
    D. cheese

11. Of the following, the BEST source of vitamins is

    A. injections
    B. capsules
    C. tablets
    D. foods

12. The two elements MOST vitally concerned with the building of red blood cells are

    A. calcium and potassium
    B. iron and copper
    C. sodium and sulfur
    D. chlorine and phosphorous

13. Two minerals present in combined form in the bones and teeth are

    A. calcium and phosphorous
    B. iron and chlorine
    C. sodium and iron
    D. potassium and magnesium

14. Yeast contains all of the following EXCEPT

    A. ascorbic acid
    B. riboflavin
    C. thiamin
    D. niacin

15. Carotene is changed to vitamin A CHIEFLY in the

    A. liver
    B. pancreas
    C. small intestine
    D. large intestine

16. Foods which ordinarily will NOT start the process of dental decay are

    A. cakes
    B. carbonated beverages
    C. meats
    D. preserves

17. The term *trace elements* is applied to

    A. the use of patch tests to determine allergies
    B. minerals present in foods in very small amounts
    C. hereditary factors
    D. symptomatic indications of illnesses

18. The exchange of oxygen and carbon dioxide between inspired air and the blood takes place in the

   A. bronchioles
   B. alveoli
   C. arterioles
   D. villi

19. Of the following associations of the number of vertebrae and area of the spinal column, the INCORRECT one is:

   A. Cervical - 7
   B. Thoracic - 10
   C. Lumbar - 5
   D. Sacrum - 5

20. A carbuncle is a(n)

   A. collection of boils in one spot
   B. ringworm infection due to a fungus
   C. infection of a hair follicle
   D. inflammation of the oil glands

21. A deviated septum is NOT associated with

   A. impaired breathing
   B. hoarseness
   C. post-nasal drip
   D. malocclusion

22. The cervical and lumbar spinal curves

   A. are in opposite directions to each other
   B. are inflexible
   C. are present at birth
   D. result from the efforts of the child to assume the upright position

23. All of the following are necessary for proper seating EXCEPT that the student's

   A. lumbar region of the spine should be supported by the back of the chair
   B. feet should rest squarely on the floor
   C. hips should be pushed back in the chair as far as possible
   D. knees should be firmly supported by the forward edge of the seat

24. All of the following conditions are considered to be deviations of the spine EXCEPT

   A. scoliosis   B. keratosis   C. lordosis   D. kyphosis

25. All of the following associations are correct EXCEPT:

   A. Ankle - hinge joint
   B. Wrist - biaxial joint
   C. Hip - ball-and-socket joint
   D. Knee - pivot joint

KEY (CORRECT ANSWERS)

1.	B	11.	D
2.	C	12.	B
3.	B	13.	A
4.	C	14.	A
5.	D	15.	A
6.	A	16.	C
7.	B	17.	B
8.	D	18.	B
9.	D	19.	B
10.	B	20.	A

21. D
22. D
23. D
24. B
25. D

TEST 3

DIRECTIONS: Each question or incomplete statement is followed by several suggested answers or completions. Select the one that BEST answers the question or completes the statement. *PRINT THE LETTER OF THE CORRECT ANSWER IN THE SPACE AT THE RIGHT.*

1. The gland that maintains harmony among the body functions by its control and coordination of the other endocrine glands is the   1.____

    A. thyroid   B. pituitary   C. adrenals   D. pineal

2. The maintenance of body balance is MOST closely associated with the   2.____

    A. eustachian tube   B. ear drum
    C. semi-circular canals   D. stapes

3. The terms endomorph, mesomorph, and ectomorph relate to   3.____

    A. extreme varieties of human physique
    B. digestive organs
    C. muscular system
    D. subcutaneous tissues

4. Even if an individual has lost the use of the pectoralis major, he is able to perform all of the following actions EXCEPT to   4.____

    A. employ power in forward and downward movements of the arm
    B. raise his hand to any position in front of the trunk
    C. fold his arms
    D. place the hand on the opposite shoulder

5. The muscle which depresses the humerus, draws it backward, and rotates it inward is the   5.____

    A. deltoid   B. trapezius
    C. latissimus dorsi   D. biceps

6. All of the following statements are correct EXCEPT: 6.____

    A. Striated voluntary cells are found in muscles of the arm
    B. Smooth involuntary cells are found in the walls of the alimentary canal
    C. Smooth voluntary cells are found in muscles of the eye
    D. Striated involuntary cells are found in the heart muscle

7. An example of a vestigial structure in the human body is   7.____

    A. a sweat gland   B. the appendix
    C. the pineal gland   D. a kidney

8. An example of an anti-peristaltic movement is   8.____

    A. blushing   B. swallowing
    C. relaxing   D. vomiting

95

9. The vision by which a baseball player stealing second base can see not only the player covering the base but others indirectly approaching the base is called _____ vision.

   A. tunnel
   B. barrel
   C. peripheral
   D. functional

10. For an individual with weak posture, the recumbent position for exercise is easier than the standing position because of all of the following reasons EXCEPT that, in the recumbent position, the

    A. effort in maintaining balance is relatively less
    B. gravity assists the body to be more at rest
    C. individual is less likely to fatigue
    D. heart and respiratory rates are increased, thus creating a better physiological approach to muscle action

11. All of the following are types of faulty posture occurring in the anteroposterior plane EXCEPT

    A. stoop shoulders
    B. round back
    C. high right shoulder
    D. hollow back

12. Sedentary occupations are MOST frequently associated with

    A. overdeveloped trapezius muscles
    B. strong rhomboid muscles
    C. increased tone and strength of the pectoral muscles
    D. powerful erector spinal muscles

13. When treating wounds, it is IMPORTANT to remember that

    A. puncture wounds can cause tetanus
    B. lacerations and punctures are the most serious
    C. the danger of tetanus is possible in all wounds
    D. wounds which bleed are more serious than those which don't bleed

14. Fractures of bones may be classified as

    A. comminuted, simple, and closed
    B. compound, simple, and comminuted
    C. comminuted, contaminated, and open
    D. simple, compound, and closed

15. When a product is advertised as having many curative powers, it is called a

    A. placebo
    B. panacea
    C. nostrum
    D. proprietary medicine

16. The MOST serious danger associated with quackery in the treatment of health problems is that it

    A. may delay medical treatment until it is too late
    B. leads to incompetent persons obtaining money falsely
    C. leads to false hope by the patient
    D. involves many innocent people who are *used* by the quack

17. A state program of medical assistance to needy persons which is financed by state and federal governments is

    A. Medicare
    B. Medicaid
    C. Blue Cross-Blue Shield
    D. Health Insurance Plan

18. *Nader's Raiders* activities brought about much-needed reforms in the

    A. Federal Trade Commission
    B. Food and Drug Administration
    C. Department of Health, Education, and Welfare
    D. Hazardous Substances Act

19. The system of healing that is based on the manipulation of the spine is

    A. chiropractic
    B. naturopathy
    C. osteoptics
    D. ophthalmology

20. More leisure time, labor saving devices, spectator sports, and automation have increased the incidence of the medical problem of

    A. obesity
    B. diabetes
    C. high blood pressure
    D. strokes

21. Man does NOT contract most animal diseases because he has

    A. acquired immunity
    B. passive immunity
    C. immune serum
    D. natural immunity

22. Bones and teeth of children are strengthened by foods rich in

    A. potassium and iodine
    B. potassium and iron
    C. calcium and phosphorus
    D. calcium and chlorine

23. A student with a non-functioning gall bladder will have difficulty digesting

    A. fats   B. sugars   C. starches   D. proteins

24. During the digestive process, amino acids are produced primarily from

    A. fats
    B. carbohydrates
    C. vitamins
    D. proteins

25. The chemical element MOST often found to be deficient in both city and country diets is

    A. iron   B. calcium   C. iodine   D. sodium

KEY (CORRECT ANSWERS)

1.	B	11.	C
2.	C	12.	C
3.	A	13.	A
4.	A	14.	D
5.	C	15.	B
6.	C	16.	A
7.	B	17.	B
8.	D	18.	A
9.	C	19.	A
10.	D	20.	A

21. D
22. C
23. A
24. D
25. A

TEST 4

DIRECTIONS: Each question or incomplete statement is followed by several suggested answers or completions. Select the one that BEST answers the question or completes the statement. *PRINT THE LETTER OF THE CORRECT ANSWER IN THE SPACE AT THE RIGHT.*

1. The sources of saturated fats are

   A. meats and cereals
   B. fish and vegetable oils
   C. vegetables and meats
   D. meats and dairy products

   1.____

2. The energy required for the body to maintain its internal life process is called

   A. basal metabolism
   B. metabolic rate
   C. nutritional requirement
   D. caloric balance

   2.____

3. In the exercise of *double leg lifting* while in a supine position, the abdominal muscles act as

   A. stabilizers
   B. prime movers
   C. neutralizers
   D. assistant movers

   3.____

4. The vastus medialis and the popliteus are muscles primarily involved with movement of the

   A. elbow   B. knee   C. neck   D. hip

   4.____

5. The CORRECT association is:

   A. sartorius - chest
   B. gastrocnemius - leg
   C. trapezius - foot
   D. pectoralis minor - back

   5.____

6. Exercises for those with chronic heart conditions should

   A. consist of isometrics
   B. be completely eliminated
   C. consist of simple, light movements
   D. be mildly competitive

   6.____

7. The amount of water eliminated daily through perspiration by the average person is APPROXIMATELY _____ quart(s).

   A. 2 to 3
   B. 4 to 5
   C. $\frac{1}{2}$ to 1
   D. none of the above

   7.____

8. Floor or scuff *burns* are examples of _____ wounds.

   A. abrasion
   B. puncture
   C. laceration
   D. incision

   8.____

9. When applying an arm sling in cases of injury to the hand or lower forearm, the sling should be adjusted so that the hand is

   9.____

A. completely covered
B. four inches above the level of the elbow
C. on the same level as the elbow
D. six inches below the level of the elbow

10. The first aid procedure for strains is to

    A. massage the affected part vigorously
    B. apply warm, moist applications
    C. immediately immobilize the affected part
    D. bandage tightly to restrict movement

10.____

11. In all fracture cases, the IMMEDIATE objective of the first aider is to

    A. try to set the bone
    B. move the victim to a more comfortable position
    C. prevent further damage
    D. take the victim to a doctor or hospital

11.____

12. When fluid accumulates between the epidermis and dermis following irritation of a local area, a _____ has formed.

    A. callous   B. boil   C. corn   D. blister

12.____

13. Of the following, the food HIGHEST in calorie value per pound is

    A. lamb   B. chocolate   C. butter   D. sugar

13.____

14. Of the following foods, the one contributing MOST to growth and repair of tissue is

    A. bread
    B. honey
    C. string beans
    D. cheese

14.____

15. Of the following types of wounds, the one considered MOST dangerous from the point of view of infection is the

    A. laceration
    B. abrasion
    C. puncture
    D. incision

15.____

16. Of the following, the MOST characteristic symptom of a third degree burn is

    A. the skin is blistered
    B. there is deep destruction of tissue
    C. the skin is reddened
    D. the skin is charred

16.____

17. The medical term for *hardening of the arteries* is

    A. carcinoma
    B. arthritis
    C. thrombosis
    D. arteriosclerosis

17.____

18. The process of destroying micro-organisms which cause disease or infection is called

    A. contamination
    B. immunization
    C. inoculation
    D. sterilization

18.____

19. Carpus, ethmoid, and coccyx are

    A. arteries   B. bones   C. enzymes   D. ligaments

20. The quality of a protein food and its effectiveness in body building are determined by the

    A. amount of corrective tissue it contains
    B. number and amount of the amino acids it contains
    C. acid-forming elements it contains
    D. amount of water present in the food

21. All of the following are found in vitamin B complex EXCEPT

    A. nicotinic acid   B. riboflavin
    C. thiamine   D. prothrombin

22. All of the following associations are correct EXCEPT:

    A. Sedative - quiets activity
    B. Analgesic - produces insensibility to pain
    C. Soporific - stimulates
    D. Anodyne - relieves pain

23. Sickle cell anemia is a blood disease MOST commonly found in children whose parents are

    A. Caucasian   B. interracial
    C. black or Latin American   D. oriental

24. In order to determine the basal metabolic rate of an individual, all of the following conditions must be included EXCEPT that the

    A. environment temperature must be comfortably warm
    B. test must be made from 12 to 18 hours after the last meal
    C. body must be in the waking state and at complete rest
    D. test should be preceded by a ten-minute period of vigorous exercise

25. The accumulation of an oxygen debt by a normally healthy individual engaged in sport activity is related MOST directly to

    A. lack of endurance
    B. limited residual air
    C. strenuous exercise
    D. failure of the hemoglobin to combine with oxygen

KEY (CORRECT ANSWERS)

1.	D	11.	C
2.	A	12.	D
3.	A	13.	C
4.	B	14.	D
5.	B	15.	C
6.	C	16.	B
7.	A	17.	D
8.	A	18.	D
9.	B	19.	B
10.	B	20.	B

21. D
22. C
23. C
24. D
25. C

THERAPISTS

CAREER DESCRIPTIONS

CONTENTS

		Page
I.	Art Therapist	1
II.	Athletic Trainer	3
III.	Corrective Therapist	4
IV.	Dance Therapist	6
V.	Horticultural Therapist	8
VI.	Manual Arts Therapist	9
VII.	Music Therapist	10
VIII.	Occupational Therapist	12
IX.	Occupational Therapist Assistant	15
X.	Orthotic-Prosthetic Technician	16
XI.	Orthotist	17
XII.	Physical Therapist	18
XIII.	Physical Therapy Assistant	20
XIV.	Prosthetist	20
XV.	Recreation Therapist	22
XVI.	Speech Pathologist and Audiologist	23
XVII.	Vocational Rehabilitation Counselor	24

THERAPISTS

CAREER DESCRIPTIONS

The primary objective of therapy is helping individuals with physical, mental, or social handicaps to regain their capacity for self-help and independence. To meet this goal, different kinds of therapists are employed, each with special knowledge and skills which can be used in rehabilitation. For example, art, dance, and music therapists bring both artistic and therapeutic skills to their work and try to improve the mental and physical well-being of their patients. Dance and art techniques are used as nonverbal means of communication, and, along with music, are often useful in helping patients to resolve physical, emotional, and social problems. Horticultural therapists use gardening, an enjoyable and relaxing activity, for such purposes as training disabled or handicapped patients, evaluating the abilities of patients, or as a social activity for patients. Corrective therapists treat their patients by using medically prescribed exercises and activities. Physical therapists work with persons who are physically disabled by illness, accident, or birth defects. They use exercise and such treatments as heat, cold, and electricity to improve the patient's condition.

Occupational therapists help individuals with physical or emotional disabilities by teaching daily living skills or job skills. On the other hand, manual arts therapists use industrial arts such as graphics or wood and metalworking to rehabilitate their patients. Recreation therapists use sports, games, crafts, camping, and hobbies as part of the rehabilitation of ill, disabled, or handicapped persons. Athletic trainers care for and try to prevent injuries of individuals engaged in professional, amateur, and school athletics.

Persons whose limbs are lost or disabled through injury, disease, or birth defects require highly skilled and specialized services, provided by orthotists and prosthetists. Orthotists make and fit orthopedic braces, while prosthetists make and fit artificial limbs.

Speech pathologists and audiologists work with children and adults who have speech, language, or hearing impairments. Rehabilitation counselors help persons with physical, mental, or social problems return to or begin a normal life by obtaining satisfactory work.

It is obvious that therapy and related activities offer a broad area for career exploration by interested individuals, and in the following pages each of the specializations mentioned briefly here is treated in greater detail.

I. **ART THERAPIST**
    Activity Therapist
    Art Psychotherapist
    Art Specialist

Expressing personal ideas through art and achieving some sense of well-being as a result is a very old concept. Pictures have been found scratched or painted on the cave walls of primitive man, and many ancient tools and objects were designed not only to be useful but also artistically pleasing. Exactly what made the cave dwellers and their ancestors draw the pictures or design the objects is not known, but it can be assumed that they must have received some sort of emotional satisfaction from creating them. This is the basis of art therapy which, simply stated, uses the concept of art as a device for non-verbal expression and communication. Art therapy attempts to resolve the individual's emotional conflicts and encourages personal growth and self-understanding.

The most practical application of art therapy has been with those suffering from mental disorders, mental handicapped, or other problems of social and psychological development, but innovative work has also been done on a variety of other problems. Art therapists confer with members of the medical health team to diagnose patients' problems. Combining art, education, and insight, art therapists assess their patients' problems, strengths, and weaknesses and determine a course of treatment best suited to accomplish specific treatment goals. Art therapists plan art activities, maintain and distribute supplies and materials, provide art instruction, and observe and record the various relationships that occur during therapy sessions. Emphasis is not placed on the quality of the product, but rather on the well-being of the patient. Art therapists often work as members of teams of other professionals and coordinate their activities with those of other therapists.

Art therapists work with people of all ages who have varying degrees of impairment or with normal populations in schools and growth centers. They may practice with individuals, groups, and/or families in clinical, educational, or rehabilitative settings which include private psychiatric hospitals and clinics, community health centers, geriatric centers, drug and alcohol clinics, nursing homes, halfway houses, prisons, public and private schools, and institutions for the emotionally disturbed, learning disabled, brain damaged, deaf, blind, physically handicapped, and multiple disabled. Many art therapists who work in clinics also teach art therapy in colleges or universities, and may do research in some aspect of therapy. However, the primary involvement of most art therapists is with clients in some type of clinical setting. Art therapists normally work a 40-hour week, although the hours and degree of responsibility vary with the setting. The facilities they work in are usually fully equipped with art materials, tables, chairs, art desks, and storage areas, and in general the working conditions are good.

Job Requirements

Entry into the field of art therapy at the professional level requires a master's degree or its equivalent in institutional training. Undergraduate work in the fine arts and the behavioral and social sciences is not only desirable but, in most instances, required for entry into the master's program. An undergraduate program specifically planned to lead to a degree in art therapy would be even more helpful. Training is offered at a number of schools, clinical facilities, and other institutions located throughout the United States.

Licensure is not required for art therapists unless they work in public schools. In such cases, they must be licensed in the state in which they plan to work. The American Art Therapy Association, Inc. has established a national registry for art therapists, and to be accepted for registration with the association the applicant must meet certain experience and educational requirements. A master's degree in art therapy and 1 year of work experience will satisfy the requirements, but there are also several other ways in which the requirements may be met. Specific information on other methods of meeting registration standards can be obtained from the association. Registration is not always required for employment, but each year more employers are asking for this credential.

Opportunities

The employment outlook for qualified art therapists is favorable, and opportunities in this field are expected to grow.

There are no uniform paths of advancement for art therapists. Promotion may take many forms including assuming additional responsibility, administering an art therapy project, or moving into a specialty field such as special education, psychotherapy, or drug counseling. In most instances, promotions are based on experience and/or additional training.

II. ATHLETIC TRAINER
Certified Athletic Trainer

Athletic trainers are professionally trained medical technicians who work in conjunction with and under the supervision of a physician. They are responsible for the prevention and care of injuries usually associated with competitive athletics. They administer immediate first aid to injured athletes and carry out treatment and rehabilitation procedures prescribed by the team physician. They also keep the teach coach informed of the injured athletes' condition.

Trainers' duties include taking care of minor injuries such as cuts, scratches, abrasions, and blisters; making protective devices such as mouthpieces and injury pads; and taping, wrapping, and padding injuries. Trainers must be skilled in massage and corrective-exercise techniques and be able to use therapeutic equipment such as diathermy units, whirlpools, infrared lamps, and ultrasound machines. Athletic trainers also conduct conditioning and rehabilitation programs; plan menus and supervise diets; and aid in purchasing and fitting equipment. Some athletic trainers also make travel and menu arrangements for traveling teams. Since many athletic trainers are employed by educational institutions, including secondary and higher education facilities, they often teach classes in related or nonrelated subjects as part of their regular duties.

Most athletic trainers work in secondary schools, colleges, or universities, and a limited number are employed by professional athletic teams. The nature of the work requires athletic trainers to work long and irregular hours. It is not uncommon for trainers to work 55 or more hours per week. Emergencies and illnesses which require their attention may come up at any time, and the regular schedule includes any of the days and evenings of the week, often including holidays. Travel can be part of the job and is a necessity for trainers who work with a professional team, which may be away from home for long periods of time.

Job Requirements

The educational minimum for entry into this work is a bachelor's degree in athletic training, but an increasing number of candidates have graduate training. The certifying agency for programs in athletic training is the National Athletic Trainers Association (NATA). Typical courses of study include anatomy, physiology, physiology of exercise, kinesiology, physics, chemistry, psychology, first aid, safety, nutrition, administration of health and physical education programs, and techniques of athletic training. In addition, the program may lead to teaching certification in physical or health education.

Certification by the National Athletic Trainers Association (NATA) is not required to obtain employment, but it is considered to be a valuable credential in this field. To become a certified athletic trainer, an individual must meet a number of requirements, including having a college degree with specified courses and a teaching license.

Opportunities

At present, most opportunities exist in learning institutions. However, future demand in these positions may be determined to a large extent by federal legislation which, if introduced and passed, will require each school to employ an athletic trainer. Currently, the trainer with the best employment potential for these jobs is also able to teach a subject or subjects for which there is a demand. The more subjects the trainer is able to teach, the greater the chances for employment. Some athletic trainer positions require individual trainers to serve a group of schools or an entire school district. Under this arrangement, the trainer is usually located in a central place, such as a stadium, and has a small staff which provides the schools with an athletic trainer and facilities. In some cases, trainers take teaching positions in which they teach the skills of the profession to other athletic trainers. Competition is keenest for positions with professional athletic teams, and chances of starting a career as a professional trainer are very slim.

Advancement in this career is regulated by the employing institution or team and, although there are no set patterns of advancement, a number of possibilities exist. One would be to start as an assistant athletic trainer, progress to trainer, and then to head trainer or director of training. A trainer at an educational institution might work into an athletic administration position. The athletic trainer whose employment is with a professional team is in a somewhat special employment situation. Usually, the professional trainer works only with one sport. Although most professional teams operate only approximately 6 months a year, they have an off-season program and employ the trainer during the full year.

III. CORRECTIVE THERAPIST
Adapted Physical Educator
Therapeutic Exercise Specialist

Corrective therapists treat patients by using medically prescribed physical exercises and activities which strengthen and coordinate body functions and prevent muscular deterioration caused by inactivity due to illness. They apply the principles, tools, techniques, and psychology of medically oriented physical education to help persons with physical and mental problems meet their treatment goals. Therapists design or adjust equipment and devise exercises to meet the needs of patients. They instruct patients in proper exercise techniques and equipment usage to meet specific objectives such as walking, joint flexibility, endurance, strength, or emotional self-confidence and security. For the physically handicapped, the exercise routines are aimed at developing strength, dexterity, and coordination of muscles. Therapists teach exercise routines to wheelchair patients, instruct amputees or partially paralyzed patients how to walk and move around, and sometimes give driving lessons to handicapped persons using specially equipped automobiles. They also advise patients on the use of braces, artificial limbs, and other devices. For the emotionally ill or mentally handicapped, they use exercises to relieve frustration or tension, or to bring about social involvement.

Corrective therapists also judge strength, endurance, and self-care ability to gage the patient's recovery at successive stages. Corrective therapists participate in staff planning sessions and make ward rounds as members of health-care teams. They prepare progress reports on patient responses to therapeutic treatment exercises and present findings orally or in writing at staff meetings and conferences. Corrective therapists also counsel members of the patients' families on therapeutic matters. Corrective therapy should not be confused with physical therapy. Physical therapists employ physical agents such as heat, water, and light in treatment routines, and perform tests to determine nerve, muscle, and skin condition and reaction. Corrective therapy is used mainly in the more advanced stages of rehabilitation where functional training is required.

Some corrective therapists choose areas of specialization in this field. Corrective therapists who specialize in driver training are concerned with teaching handicapped persons safe driving methods, developing their remaining skills, and teaching them to use special driving devices. Seminars and workshops in driver training are required for this specialization and therapists working in this area are primarily employed by the Veterans Administration. Corrective therapists who specialize in cardiac rehabilitation are concerned with conducting programs of cardiorespiratory rehabilitation which entail checking patients' pulmonary levels, establishing work performance limits, and establishing levels of progression to attain optimal fitness capabilities. Workers receive specialized training in cardiopulmonary theory, methodology and techniques, and the use of specialized equipment. Some corrective therapists are beginning to specialize in therapeutic exercise activities which are conducted in therapeutic pools in numerous hospital and health-education sites. This specialization requires water safety certifications, such as those given by the Red Cross or YMCA/YWCA, and knowledge of effects of water activities and effects of water on exercise performance.

Corrective therapists work in a variety of government, public, and private facilities, including hospitals, rehabilitation clinics, schools, colleges, and universities, nursing homes, special schools, recreation facilities, and camps for the handicapped. They work a 40-hour week, usually in an indoor setting although outdoor recreation areas and pools are also used. There are a variety of physical demands involved in being a corrective therapist, such as demonstrating exercises and equipment use, lifting and balancing patients, and handling and adjusting therapeutic-exercise equipment.

Job Requirements

A high school student considering a career in corrective therapy can plan on spending at least 4 years in obtaining a bachelor's degree in physical education from an accredited college or university. In addition to completing degree requirements, prospective corrective therapists must also complete a 400-hour clinical internship at an approved institution. Courses taken as part of the degree requirements, or in addition to them, include medical orientation courses in neurology, pathology, therapeutic exercise, developmental psychology, psychology of the exceptional/atypical, kinesiology, advanced anatomy, neuromuscular re-education, and physiological psychology. Many of these courses are required for a master's degree, and while this level of education is not required for entry into the field, it is considered an asset in seeking both entry level and promotional positions.

There are no State licensure requirements for corrective therapists at this time. However, therapists are eligible for certification if they meet the requirements set by the American Corrective Therapy Association. Requirements for certification include a bachelor's degree in physical education, specific medical/therapeutic orientation courses, 400 hours of clinical training experience, and a satisfactory score on the certification examination. While certification is snot normally considered a condition of employment, it is considered advantageous since it indicates that the therapist has met the standards set by the association. The association also encourages its membership to enroll in continuing education courses as a means of improving professional growth and development.

Opportunities

The employment opportunities for corrective therapists are favorable. There is also the prospect of future growth and expansion in the profession as the importance of corrective therapists in rehabilitation is recognized to a greater degree and increases in government funding of programs occur.

Advancement to supervisory or administrative positions is possible for qualified therapists. Promotions are generally based on work experience, level of skill, and the completion of advanced education courses. Therapists in government facilities can advance through the traditional civil service methods.

IV. DANCE THERAPIST
Dance/Movement Therapist
Movement Therapist
Psychomotor Therapist

For centuries dancing and related types of body movement have been recognized and used not only as a form of entertainment but also as a way to ease tension and obtain other physical and emotional benefits. To many, this type of physical activity produces a renewal of emotional well-being, a means of self-expression, and a recharging of energy that has been drained away by the frustrations of everyday living. In this sense, dancing and body movement are therapeutic activities. A practical application for use with individuals who have emotional and often physical impairments caused by injury, illness, or birth defects has been developed by dance therapists who use dance and body movement as a tool to further emotional and physical integration and well-being. They take advantage of the expressive and communicative aspects of dance to help people resolve social, emotional, and physical disorders.

Dance therapists make an assessment of their client's emotional and social behavior, movement capabilities, and general posture. They then determine what types of movement experiences will best help the client to develop an increased awareness of feelings and non-verbal behavior, a wider, closer interaction of mind and body, an improved body image, improved social relations, and relief from physical and emotional blocks. Working with individuals and groups, dance therapists plan and conduct movement sessions designed to achieve those goals and objectives that they have worked out with their clients. In many instances, dance therapists also work in cooperation with other mental health professionals. They discuss client goals and progress to coordinate treatment activities and work toward overall objectives. Dance therapists also participate in case conferences, staff meetings, community meetings, verbal therapy sessions, and other activities, depending on the setting in which they work. Some engage in research on movement behavior, teach or train others in educational or employment settings, or act as consultants to various agencies or organizations. While there are many varieties of dance therapy settings, only one real area of specialization exists: movement research. The movement researcher observes, records, and analyzes nonverbal behavior in live settings, on videotape, or on film. In addition to the general knowledge and experience required of the dance therapist, the movement researcher must have completed advance courses in movement observation and research methods.

Dance therapists work in a variety of mental-health settings, including psychiatric hospitals, clinics, day-care centers, community mental-health centers, developmental centers, correctional facilities, special schools, substance-abuse programs, and facilities for the aged. Registered dance therapists may also work in private practice or teach in educational facilities. Hours and other working conditions vary, as do the facilities themselves. Some are modern and well equipped, while others are older and sometimes quite sparse in terms of equipment and other things that contribute to pleasant work/therapy setting. Most aspects of the work involve close physical contact with different types of patient groups, as well as a good deal of physical activity. In all instances, strength, flexibility, stamina, and a strong desire to relate to and help others are necessary.

Job Requirements

There are two basic ways in which an individual may prepare for a career as a dance therapist. The first is the master's degree from a program in dance therapy, which will be required for registry by the American Dance Therapy Association (ADTA) and is currently recommended by that association as the professional level of training. The alternate way is a master's degree in a related field (e.g., psychology) with intensive training in the theory and practice of dance therapy and internship experience.

Neither method of preparation requires specific high school courses, but dance training in a broad range of techniques is strongly preferred. The minimum preprofessional training includes a B.S. or B.A. degree with extensive training in a variety of dance forms, course work in psychology and other social sciences, anatomy, and kinesiology. The preferred pre-professional training includes a bachelor's degree in liberal arts with emphasis in dance or psychology, courses in dance theory, performing and choreographic experience, experience in teaching dance to normal populations, and experience in personal psychotherapy. Either program may require a movement interview for acceptance.

The master's program in dance therapy, which is from 1½ year to 2 years in length, includes training in both theoretical and practical aspects of dance therapy. Studies emphasize using body movement to establish communication and rapport with clients and learning to observe and analyze movement behavior. Courses include practical training and dance therapy, movement observation, psychodynamics, and studies in human behavior. Supervised experience in clinical settings, field visits, and internships are also included.

The possible alternate requires a master's degree in a related field (dance, psychology, social work, etc.), at least 120 hours each of theory and practice of dance therapy, and course work in group dynamics, anatomy and kinesiology, and techniques of observing and assessing movement behavior. A 700 hour clinical internship, supervised by a registered dance therapist, is also required. The disadvantage of this type of program is that it may lack the coherence and integration of a master's degree program in dance therapy. It is useful for those who already have a master's degree in a related field and can complete the other required course work before September.

There are no licensing requirements for this work, and most employers do not require registration or certification. However, the American Dance Therapy Association (ADTA) has established a registry to insure professional standards of training and practice. Registration with this association is needed to work in private practice and to train dance therapy students. It may also be preferred by many employers, especially if there is a dance therapy internship program in existence at the facility or projected for the future, but there are no laws which require registration for employment. To qualify for registry with the ADTA at present, there are several requirements which must be met. Generally, they include membership in the ADTA; a bachelor's degree (a master degree) with prescribed education, training, and experience requirements; 2 years of paid experience with work in several specific areas of dance therapy; and a written description of a therapy session showing an integration of dance therapy and practice.

Opportunities

At present, dance therapy jobs are in short supply, but several factors may influence this situation, including a growing interest in nonverbal communication; awareness of the importance of body image in mental health and education; and the maintenance of high training standards. If each of these factors remain constant or accelerate and money is available, demand for dance therapists in all areas should open up. However, interested individuals should check available openings in their areas and contact the professional association to get a detailed report of local labor market conditions.

In most cases, advancement possibilities in this field are determined by the requirements of the employing facility and standards and practices vary greatly. However, a master's degree and paid work experience are factors given heavy consideration for promotion to senior clinical positions in most facilities. Teaching or administrative skills are also quite useful for purposes of advancement.

V. HORTICULTURAL THERAPIST
Garden Therapist
Hort-therapist

Horticultural therapists use horticultural activities as the primary treatment method to bring about a beneficial change in an individual with a physical, mental, or social handicap. They use gardening for a variety of purposes, such as to rehabilitate patients after illness or injury; train impaired, disabled, and handicapped persons, evaluate patients' disabilities and capabilities; and provide a social activity for physically and mentally impaired persons.

Horticultural therapists organize indoor or outdoor programs for patients with different types of problems and usually do so in a group setting. They use plant materials to help handicapped individuals improve their emotional attitudes through a change in self-concept, their social skills through nonthreatening relations with others, their physical skills through activities requiring both gross and fine motor coordination, and their mental skills. Horticultural therapists work closely with other staff members to design and conduct the program suited to the needs of the particular client. In some programs, particularly those related to vocational rehabilitation, the plants may be sold, and in this situation the therapist may also have some business responsibilities. In addition to working directly with patients, horticultural therapists often teach at local colleges or universities and conduct workshops and other training programs.

Most horticultural therapists work in public or private facilities for the handicapped, including convalescent homes, juvenile centers, schools and training centers for the mentally handicapped, psychiatric hospitals, and general-care hospitals. Horticultural therapists work closely with both people and plants, and the work setting is often a greenhouse or outside garden. Care of plants can be demanding, and the ability to move the hands easily and skillfully is very important. However, there are no physical requirements for the job, and handicapped individuals may, in fact, have the advantage of serving as role models for patients.

Job Requirements

Degrees in horticultural therapy are offered by colleges of agriculture and departments of horticulture and forestry in a number of universities. There are four levels of degrees in horticultural therapy; associate of arts, bachelor of science, master of science, and a doctorate. The length of training varies with the student's academic goal, which may be an associate degree leading to a position as a horticultural therapy aide or a bachelor of science degree which leads to a position as horticultural therapist. The training program consists of a horticulture curriculum with courses related to therapy as a specialization, plus internship and field studies.

At this time horticultural therapists are registered under a voluntary registration procedure administered by the National Council for Therapy and Rehabilitation through Horticulture. Neither registration nor continuing education is required at this time; however, all practitioners are strongly encouraged to participate.

Opportunities

Since this is a very new professional field, it is difficult to make accurate projections as to future occupational opportunities. However, the experience of the National Council for Therapy and Rehabilitation auspices of the Office of Education (HEW) indicate that the potential for jobs in this field is excellent and will continue to increase in the future.

Most horticultural therapy programs today are new and small, but they show signs of rapid growth. As programs increase in size, the opportunities for supervisory and other higher level positions are expected to expand. In addition, therapists who complete advanced training and education can obtain teaching positions in their field.

VI. MANUAL ARTS THERAPIST
Compensated Work Therapist
Incentive Therapist
Industrial Therapist
Recreation Specialist (Military)
Sheltered Workshop Supervisor
Vocational Therapist
Work Evaluator

Manual Arts therapists use mechanical, technical, and industrial activities which are vocationally significant to assist patients in their recovery and in maintaining, improving, or developing work skills. Under the direction of a physician, manual arts therapists develop a program of actual or simulated work situations which help patients to prepare for an early return to their communities as well as to the world of work.

In rehabilitation, manual arts therapists apply clinical techniques for treating the physical or mental conditions of their patients, observe their behavior, assist in their adjustment to work situations, and evaluate their manual abilities and work skills. The primary purpose is to engage patients in therapeutic activities which absorb them and help in their recovery, giving them a sense of confidence and achievement. At the same time, these work activities have a practical value since they serve to retrain patients in their own skills or trades or, where disability makes this impossible, to help them explore and learn new work skills or avocational activities.

Manual arts therapists cooperate with all members of the rehabilitation team to plan and organize work activities, considering the patient's disabilities and capabilities. Manual arts therapy may be the only therapy prescribed for a patient, or it may be used together with other therapies in a combined treatment program. It may be prescribed at any stage in the hospitalization, depending on the patient's condition and rehabilitation goals.

Patients may explore various work activities offered in manual arts therapy, including woodworking, metal working, electronics, printing and graphic arts, and sometimes agriculture. For example, a construction worker who has lost a leg in a fall may discover an interest in drawing and be taught technical drafting. A bedridden patient may learn basic electricity by using batteries and simple hookups and later advance to electronics. A patient in a wheelchair may explore jewelry or watch repair. A group of mental patients may help maintain hospital grounds. It is the job of the manual arts therapist to observe, evaluate, and guide the patients in their work activities toward their rehabilitation goals.

Manual arts therapists prepare reports describing patients' emotional and social adjustment and physical performance and work tolerance. These reports are used by the rehabilitation team in judging the progress of patients and their ability to meet the physical and mental demands of their place in the community and in the world of work.

The majority of manual arts therapists are employed in hospitals and centers operated by the Veterans Administration, but they also work in sheltered workshops, mental health clinics, workmen's compensation rehabilitation centers for the blind. The federal law requiring schooling for all handicapped children has opened a new field. Therapists normally work indoors from 8:00 A.M. to 4:30 P.M. 5 days a week, do little traveling, and generally have good working conditions. Because of the workshop setting, some noise, dust, and fumes are normally present, but these factors are usually controlled.

Job Requirements

The minimum qualification for employment in this field is a bachelor's degree in industrial arts or manual arts therapy. In addition, candidates must complete clinical training lasting several months during which the student trainees work with fully qualified therapists and participate under supervision in a treatment program. Clinical training is usually given in hospitals or rehabilitation centers affiliated with colleges.

The American Associate for Rehabilitation Therapy is the professional society for manual arts therapists and sponsors the Registry of Medical Rehabilitation Therapists and Specialists. The registry requires that a therapist be employed for 1 year in the field before being eligible for registration. Registry and membership in the association is not a condition for employment but both are considered desirable, because of opportunities for continuing education by attending seminars, meetings, and conferences, and pre-professional growth by exchange of information with other professionals.

Opportunities

The employment outlook for manual arts therapists is average, and with the current growth in rehabilitation, the demand for manual arts therapists is expected to increase slightly. The largest single employer is the Veterans Administration, with entry through the federal civil service system. Manual arts therapists may also be employed by state, local, and private facilities. Promotional opportunities in civil service are determined by specific rules; in private facilities they vary widely. Experience and competence are significant factors for promotion.

VII. MUSIC THERAPIST
Adjunctive Therapist
Creative Arts Therapist
Music Specialist
Rehabilitation Therapist
Therapeutic Activities Worker

Music has been a part of almost every culture and is recognized everywhere as having healing value. A great deal has been written about its effects and it is often described as soothing, relaxing, exciting, moving, or in terms of some other emotional feeling it creates in the listener or performer. For each individual it serves a different purpose, and for some, many purposes. For those who are disabled, music may become an actual part of medical treatment.

Music therapists have an understanding of both music and psychology and are specialists in using music as a means of accomplishing treatment goals which involve the restoration, maintenance, and improvement of mental and physical health.

In its use with the mentally ill, music therapy may achieve changes in patients' behavior that will give them new understanding of themselves and of the world around them. This can serve as a basis for improved mental health and more effective adjustment to normal living.

Often working as members of a team that may include other therapists, psychiatrists, psychologists, social workers, and special educators, music therapists make an evaluation of how a client may be helped through a music program. They determine what goals and objectives can probably be met and plan musical activities and experiences which are likely to meet them, both on an individual and group basis. Therapists treat patients of all age groups, ranging from disturbed small children and adolescents to adults who suffer from mental illness of many types and varying degrees of seriousness. As members of the mental health team, music therapists devise programs to achieve aims prescribed by attending psychiatrists, and the treatment results are evaluated periodically.

The mentally handicapped, cerebral palsied, crippled, and blind make up a group that is second only to the mentally ill in numbers receiving music therapy.

Music therapists may devise programs of many kinds in an effort to gain and to hold the patient's interest. Much depends upon the patient's potential for training, for what would be possible for one would be inappropriate for another. Group singing is commonly used. Musical appreciation and musical education is appealing to others. Every effort is made to improve skills acquired in past years and to develop an interest which will, in itself, give a new dimension to normal living.

It should be noted, however, that unlike most music programs, music therapy programs focus on the well-being of the client rather than a perfected musical product. Voice as well as traditional and nontraditional instruments are provided. In addition, instrumental and/or vocal music is often combined with body movements as a part of therapy.

Music therapists may find employment in a variety of facilities in all parts of the country. They are usually employed in psychiatric hospitals, mental handicapped centers, physical disability treatment and training institutions, day-care centers, nursing homes, special education programs, community mental health centers, special services agencies, and other related facilities.

As in many therapy situations, music therapists work very closely with their clients and must be able to relate to them and their problems in a warm professional manner. The work is not always a relaxing, pleasurable experience. The process of strengthening discipline and changing behavior can temporarily arouse anxiety and negative attitudes. Music therapists must be able to deal with these problems when they arise and use tact and resourcefulness in solving them. They often must work in close cooperation with therapists in other disciplines when physical facilities are shared to plan and schedule activities. Standard work hours are usual, but music therapists may be called on from time to time to work evening hours and weekends.

Job Requirements

The amount and type of professional training and preparation required for employment as a music therapist often varies from employer to employer, and there are people working in the field who have advanced degrees and others who are not trained in academic institutions. However, as the field grows, standard educational requirements are being more rigidly established. The minimum training and preparation currently recommended by the two associations that certify and register music therapists includes a baccalaureate degree in music therapy plus completion of a 6-month internship in an approved facility. It is to the student's advantage to attend a school which combines clinical experience and classroom work at the same time. Courses leading to the bachelor's degree in music therapy include psychology, sociology, music therapy, anthropology, music, and general education courses.

Licensure is not required of music therapists at the present time except for those working in public schools, who must be licensed as special educators in the state in which they are employed. Certification and registration may be obtained from the American Association for Music Therapists or the National Association of Music Therapists on completion of both the prescribed academic course of study at a recognized university and a 6-month clinical internship at an approved clinical-training facility. Certification and registration are not required for employment, but many employers include eligibility for them as part of their hiring policy.

Opportunities

Employment prospects depend very much on health-care trends, economic conditions, and the role of government in health care, and projections are difficult to forecast. However, today, music therapy is being used in a wider variety of treatment institutions than ever before and has been gaining acceptance as an alternate form of traditional health care. If these two trends continue, it should have a favorable influence on the demand for music therapists.

Many fields are an end in themselves, and those who enter them usually enter with the aim of making a career of performing the work they have chosen. Teaching is such a field and so is music therapy. Music therapists usually enter this career field because there is something stimulating about working with people in a therapy situation that involves music. There are rewards within the field itself and there is always the possibility of being recognized for outstanding accomplishments or for having developed new and innovative methods. Advancement is possible in this field but almost always requires the music therapist to devote less time to actual music therapy and more to administrative duties. For example, the usual path of advancement is from music therapist to department supervisor, coordinator of an activities therapy department, or other related administrative position. So, in addition to the advancement requirements of experience and/or additional education, the therapist must agree to accept an administrative position in order to be promoted. One other avenue of what might be considered advancement, but is often thought of as a separate career area, is university teaching. For a teaching position, the music therapist will need both clinical experience and a graduate degree.

VIII. OCCUPATIONAL THERAPIST
Occupational Therapist, Registered (OTR)

Occupational therapists are health professionals who provide services to all types of individuals whose lives have been impaired by physical, psychological, or developmental problems. They assist these individuals to achieve the highest level of functioning possible and to reduce or eliminate the need for continued health-care services. Like most of the other health professionals, occupational therapists usually work as a member of a medical team, which may include a physician, physical therapist, vocational counselor, and other related professionals. The team members examine the patient in terms of their individual specialties and consult with each other to arrive at an overall evaluation of the patient's capacities, skills, and abilities. Occupational therapists study those aspects of the evaluation related to occupational therapy and discuss them with the patient. Together they develop short- and long-term goals and the means by which they may be achieved. It is a complex process, and many factors are taken into consideration as a course of therapy is developed.

Therapists select appropriate activities that are suited to the physical capacity, intelligence level, and interests of each patient. These activities are designed to develop independence, prepare patients for a return to work, restore basic functions, and aid in adjustment to disabilities. The course of therapy almost always involves goal-directed activities because these activities are the primary therapy tools. For instance, occupational therapists may help patients develop an interest in ceramics, jewelry making, woodworking, weaving, or other craft activities that will improve motor skills, strength, endurance, concentration, motivation, or other physical and/or mental capacities. Other patients might be enrolled in classes which will help them prepare for specific occupational goals or develop the functional skills, abilities, and capacities needed for the tasks of everyday living.

Beside the ability to teach and to communicate with handicapped people, and a solid background of knowledge of the physical sciences and medicine, occupational therapists need specific knowledge in the various working skills used in therapy. Among these skills are leatherwork, jewelry making, ceramics, woodwork, metalwork, textile crafts, and printing. They also need to know the skills of daily living and simple homemaking. In addition to planning, directing, and participating in therapeutic goal-directed activities, occupational therapists also make and apply splints; provide patients with guidance and instruction; assist in the selection and use of equipment to help patients adapt to the environment and/or impairment; recommend changes in home or work environments to promote the patient's safety and ease of function; and determine or develop other appropriate treatments and activities. Therapists may also organize educational activities, such as the study of language or creative writing, or may organize dramatic groups. For activities such as these, they generally call upon the assistance of a professional in the particular field. Though they cannot be expert in all these activities, occupational therapists must know enough about them to understand their therapeutic values and to set them into motion.

Often physical or mental disability is so severe that patients can no longer work in their former occupations or professions. In such cases, therapists may discover some other skill or talent which patients can develop and use, and this becomes the goal of the therapy. Occupational therapists regularly prepare reports for the information of members of the health team. A report may cover, for example, an account of the progress of a physically disabled patient who has been assigned tasks of increasing difficulty. Or it may cover the progress being made by crippled children in developing muscle coordination through play with therapeutic toys.

While there are no recognized areas of specialization in this career, occupational therapists do tend to work with certain types of disability and age groups. For instance, of the occupational therapists engaged in direct service, approximately 60 percent work principally with persons who have physical disabilities and 40 percent work with patients who have psychological or emotional problems. Twenty-five percent work exclusively with persons under the age of 20, and 10 percent work exclusively with the aged. Occupational therapists are employed in a variety of facilities. Hospitals—including short- and long-term general, psychiatric, and other specialties—appear to be the major single employer of occupational therapists, employing approximately 40 percent of the total employed, while rehabilitation centers and schools each employ about 15 percent. Skilled nursing or intermediate-care facilities hire just under 10 percent, and about 5 percent find work in community mental-health programs. The remainder are scattered among private practice, home-health agencies, educational settings, day-care centers, and similar institutions. Working conditions are generally considered good but do vary among facilities. The actual range of conditions might be best described as running from adequate to excellent, but there are many factors of a highly personal nature that go into such a judgment. An individual who is interested in an occupational therapy career should visit some facilities that employ occupational therapists to form an individual opinion.

Job Requirements

Persons considering this career must be able to work with people of all kinds and all ages, with temperaments and personalities that are likely to be as varied as patient illnesses and handicaps. To gain their confidence, it is necessary to have a warm, friendly personality that inspires both trust and respect. In addition to these qualities, it is also necessary to have ingenuity and imagination in adapting activities to individual needs. The potential therapist also needs to be skilled, patient, and resourceful in teaching, since patients often present unusual and difficult learning problems. This occupation offers an excellent opportunity to combine an interest in teaching with an interest in helping people in distress and extreme need.

The educational preparation for occupational therapy requires 4 years of college training leading to the degree of bachelor of science. All occupational therapy programs offered by colleges and universities are approved by the American Medical Association's Committee on Allied Health Education and Accreditation, in collaboration with American Occupational Therapy Association.

In addition to the 4 years of academic preparation, a clinical training period is required in order to qualify for professional registration. In most schools, this clinical experience takes from 6 to 9 months.

For those who already have a degree before enrolling in a program of occupational therapy, there is an advanced-standing course of from 18 to 22 months, divided between academic and clinical work. There are also master's degree programs offered in several universities.

Although supervised clinical experience is part of all the approved programs, compensation during this period varies widely. Some institutions offer no compensation at all, others provide maintenance, and still others give a cash stipend in lieu of maintenance. The college preparation for occupational therapy emphasizes physical and behavioral sciences such as anatomy, physiology, neurology, psychology, and sociology. Other subjects include manual and creative skills, educational subjects, and recreational activities.

Graduates of accredited schools of occupational therapy are eligible to take the national registration examination conducted by the American Occupational Therapy Association. On successful completion of the examination, therapists become professionally qualified to practice and are entitled to use the initials OTR after their name. In addition to this, they automatically become certified and are eligible to become members of the association.

Opportunities

The occupational therapy profession has experienced a growth rate averaging nearly 10 percent per year. While no one can predict the future with absolute certainty, it is anticipated that employment in this occupation will continue to grow. However, the number of occupational therapy graduates is increasing every year and new graduates are expected to balance the demand created by new openings and replacement needs caused by those who leave the field for one reason or another. Therefore, there may be considerable competition for available positions, particularly in the more desirable areas. Prospective occupational therapy students are advised to check with professional occupational therapy associations, schools, and facilities that employ occupational therapists to obtain information on current needs and trends.

The usual path of advancement in this work is from staff therapist, usually the occupational therapist's first job, to senior therapist, after gaining approximately 3 years experience, to supervisor/administrative therapist, after approximately 5 years experience. Advancement, of course, is not automatic but is based on the occupational therapist's professional growth, development, and often additional education. Also, changes in this progression are not uncommon and other types of related advancement positions are possible. For instance, sometimes occupational therapists work under independent contract either providing direct occupational therapy or consulting services. Another possibility is teaching, in which the steps leading toward advancement are completely different.

IX. OCCUPATIONAL THERAPY ASSISTANT

Occupational therapy assistants work under the direction of professional occupational therapists in carrying out rehabilitation programs. They relieve the therapists of many routine tasks, allowing them to serve a greater number of patients. Therapists and assistants are partners in the rehabilitation of patients impaired by physical, psychological, or developmental problems.

Occupational therapy assistants help occupational therapists to plan and carry out educational, vocational, and recreational activities programs aimed at helping patients to regain the use of those capacities that remain after accident, disease, or deformity. They teach and assist patients to develop skills in self-care and in work-related, creative, and recreational activities. Since they work very closely with patients, occupational therapy assistants observe them and make reports to the occupational therapist on the patients' progress and development. In addition, occupational therapy assistants perform many other tasks such as ordering, preparing, and laying out materials; helping to make splints, braces, and other assistive devices; and maintaining tools and equipment. While there are no recognized specialization areas in this career, occupational therapist assistants tend to be assigned to work with certain types of disability or age group populations. For instance, one therapist may work almost exclusively with physical disabilities, another with psychological or emotional problems, a third may work exclusively with patients under 20 years of age, and a fourth may work only with the aged.

Many types of facilities located throughout the country employ occupational therapy assistants. Hospitals are the largest employer, employing about 50 percent. The remainder are divided among nursing homes, schools for handicapped children and the mentally handicapped, rehabilitation and day-care centers, clinics, and similar institutions. Working conditions are generally considered good, although they vary from facility to facility. However, since many personal factors go into making an evaluation of facilities and working conditions, the prospective occupational therapy assistant should visit several facilities that employ occupational therapy assistants to form an individual opinion.

Job Requirements

High school graduates can prepare for this career by completing a 2-year associate degree program in an accredited university or junior or community college. These programs include a minimum of 2 months of supervised practical experience. They also include courses covering structure and function of the human body, growth and development from childhood to old age, physical disability, and mental illness. In addition, there is training in therapeutic skills and crafts. Graduates of a program approved by the American Occupational Therapy Association are eligible for certification as an occupational therapy assistant (COTA) if they meet specified education and experience requirements. At present, there are no licensure requirements for occupational therapy assistants. Continuing education is not a requirement for occupational therapy assistants. However, additional course work not only keeps the assistant up to date on what is happening in the profession but helps to develop expertise, making the employee ore valuable and more qualified for promotion.

Opportunities

The demand for occupational therapy assistants is expected to continue to grow at a steady rate. The number of training programs offered by schools is also expected to increase, but the supply of graduates is expected to fall short of the demand for qualified occupational therapy assistants. The best possibilities for advancement are in the larger facilities, where assistants may be given more and more responsibilities as they gain experience. After occupational therapy assistants have completed 4 years of acceptable experience, they are eligible and may apply to take the American Occupational Therapy Association examination to become occupational therapists.

X. ORTHOTIC-PROSTHETIC TECHNICIAN

Orthotic-prosthetic technicians make, repair, and maintain orthotic and prosthetic devices, under the guidance of an orthoptist/prosthetist. Orthotic devices include braces and surgical supports, while prosthetic devices refer to such items as artificial limbs or plastic cosmetic devices. Technicians, working under the supervision of an orthoptist-prosthetist, follow prescription specifications to determine the type of device to be made and the tools and materials required. When working with orthotic devices, they bend, form, and fasten parts of metal braces to conform to measurements, using a variety of handtools. They shape plastic and metal around casts of the patients' body or limbs and cover and pad brace structures with such materials as rubber, plastic, leather, and felt.

When working on prosthetic devices, they lay out the work; mark the sizes of parts, using precision measuring instruments; and follow prescribed specifications. Using many kinds of tools and a variety of materials such as wood, plastic, metal, or fabric, they make parts to assemble into different types of prostheses.

Orthotic-prosthetic technicians are also responsible for repairing and maintaining orthoses and prostheses as directed by the orthoptist/prosthetist. Although technicians do not take part in direct patient care activities, they have the important responsibility of insuring that the workmanship and qualify of devices produced meet acceptable standards. Technicians can specialize in orthotics or in prosthetics, or, when qualified, can perform in both orthotics and prosthetics.

Job Requirements

The American Board for Certification in Orthotics and Prosthetics registers orthotic-prosthetic technicians who meet specific requirements. Candidates for registration must have at least a 10th grade education and have a minimum of 2 years of work experience in making orthoses and/or prostheses. This experience must have been obtained under the supervision of a Certified Orthotist (CO), Certified Prosthetist (CP) or a Certified Prosthetist-Orthotist (CPO). Candidates who have completed a formal educational program in orthotics or prosthetics given in an institution accredited by the board are not required to meet the experience requirements. In addition, candidates must qualify on an examination administered by the board.

Candidates who pass the technician examination in orthotics are awarded the designation of Registered Technician (Orthotics) RT (O). Candidates passing the examination in prosthetics are designated as Registered Technician (Prosthetics) RT (P). Those who pass the combined examination for orthotic-prosthetic technician receive the designation of Registered Technician (Orthotics-Prosthetics) RT (OP).

Opportunities

Employment prospects for qualified orthotic-prosthetic technicians are generally favorable and are expected to remain so during the next several years. Advancement opportunities in this field are good and are based on work experience and completion of further education and training. By meeting prescribed training and education requirements, technicians can advance to the practitioner-level positions of Certified Orthotist, Certified Prosthetist, or Certified Prosthetist-Orthotist.

XI. ORTHOTIST

Orthotists provide care to persons with limb or spine disabilities by fitting and making devices called orthoses. These devices are orthopedic braces which support weakened body parts or help to correct physical defects such as spinal deformities. Orthotists work with physicians, following physicians' prescriptions or helping to develop prescriptions for orthoses. They examine and judge patients' orthotic needs and make recommendations based on individual problems. Orthotists are responsible for designing each orthosis; selecting proper materials; and making all measurements, model changes, and layouts of designs. In addition, they are responsible for making sure that the devices fit and work properly, for making the necessary adjustments, and for teaching patients the use and care of these devices.

Orthotists maintain accurate patient records and keep up with developments in this field in order to provide patients with the best possible care. They supervise orthotic/prosthetic technicians and other laboratory workers involved in making orthoses. They lecture and teach their specialty to colleagues or others who are interested in this field or work in research activities. Some orthotists are qualified to function as prosthetists and provide patients with artificial replacements for limbs or other body parts. In such cases, they carry the professional designation of prosthetist-orthotist.

Orthotists are employed in privately-owned facilities or laboratories; rehabilitation centers; hospitals; and Federal, State and local rehabilitation agencies.

Job Opportunities

Persons considering this career area must have skillful hands, be able to work with various types of tools, and possess mechanical ability. In addition, candidates must show patience and have a responsible attitude toward their work and a concern for detail and accuracy. Candidates must also be concerned for the welfare of the disabled and be able to communicate with both patients and members of the rehabilitation team. High school courses considered useful in preparing for this career include physics, chemistry, mathematics, biology, and shop courses in metal, wood, and plastics.

The American Board for Certification in Orthotics and Prosthetics is the certifying agency for professional practitioners in this field. They set education and training standards for orthotists and administer an examination to all candidates applying for certification status. The usual method of preparing for practitioner certification is to obtain a bachelor's degree in orthotics from an accredited college or university, combined with 1 year of clinical experience. However, persons who hold an associate degree in orthotics or another area can also qualify by completing three special courses in orthotics at an accredited training facility and obtaining 2 years of clinical experience. Persons with a bachelor's degree in a different area of specialization may also qualify for practitioner certification by completing post-graduate training in orthotics, ranging in length from 4 to 8 months, combined with 1 or 2 years of acceptable work experience. The minimum educational requirement will be a bachelor's degree.

Candidates who pass the certification examination are awarded the designation of Certified Orthotist (CO). Those orthotists who are also qualified to practice as prosthetists, and who pass the examination in both specialties, are given the designation of Certified Prosthetist-Orthotist (CPO).

Opportunities

Employment opportunities for qualified orthotists are generally good and are expected to remain so during the next several years. Advancement in this field takes different forms, depending on the employment location, but is generally based on work experience and skill level. Orthotists can advance to supervisory and administrative positions, and in some cases may become self-employed as private practitioners.

XII. PHYSICAL THERAPIST
Physiotherapist

Physical therapists are health-care practitioners who plan and administer physical treatment for patients referred by a physician in order to restore bodily functions, relieve pain, and prevent disability following disease, injury, or loss of a body part. Physical therapy has value in the treatment of a wide variety of diseases and injuries, such as multiple sclerosis, nerve injuries, chest conditions, amputations, fractures, arthritis, and cerebral palsy. Initially, physical therapists review and evaluate the patient's condition and medical records, perform indicated tests or measurements, and evaluate the findings. They use the findings to establish a patient care plan which includes setting short- and long-term goals and appropriate treatment procedures for the patient. The goal of physical therapists is to help patients to reach maximum performance levels and to regain a place in society while adjusting to the limiting effects of disabilities. When meeting a patient for the first time, physical therapists, like physicians, keep in mind the importance of preparing the patient emotionally for what is to come. They must be sensitive to the problems of the patient, who is made vulnerable by disability or disease.

Since treatments may be prolonged and often require active participation, the full cooperation of patients is very important. As a first step, therefore, physical therapists familiarize themselves with the patients' personal backgrounds, as well as their medical histories, and make an effort to gain their confidence and cooperation. The therapist-patient relationship often determines success or failure in involving patients in their own treatment. This is especially true of children. When working with children, therapists must do their best to help the parents as well as children to understand the treatment.

As members of the health team, therapists help patients overcome their disabilities through the use of exercise, heat, cold, electricity, ultrasound, and massage. To carry out these tasks, therapists must have detailed knowledge of human anatomy and physiology and know what steps may be taken to correct disease and injury.

For example, in the case of children with a birth defect, physicians call upon physical therapists who may perform a muscle evaluation in order to determine the extent of the damage. On the basis of the muscle test, plans are made for the kind of physical therapy the children need. Physical therapists then carry out the plan of treatment.

In working with such children, physical therapists give the exercises that restore weakened muscles to normalcy. Treatment may include water exercises in warm baths or pools, hot packs, electricity (currents that stimulate paralyzed muscles), ultraviolet rays, and massage. When children must be fitted with braces or crutches, therapists teach walking with the aid of these appliances.

Treatment can be more effective and progress faster if patients and their families understand the purpose and plan and know just how they can help. Physical therapy services include instructing patients and their families in how to carry on prescribed treatment programs at home. They may need specific instruction in the techniques of muscle reduction or in the care and use of braces or prosthetic appliances. Physical therapists may personally conduct the treatment program or supervise a program conducted by a physical therapist assistant.

Physical therapists work in hospitals, rehabilitation centers, nursing homes, home-health agencies, public health agencies, school districts, private practices, and the armed forces. Therapists usually work closely with other people including the patient, patient's family, and other health-care practitioners. Physical therapists are generally required to be physically fit, since the practice of physical therapy requires the worker to lift, climb, stoop, stand, and kneel. Additionally, therapists should have manual dexterity, good visual acuity and hearing, and be able to communicate both orally and in writing.

Job Requirements

Adaptability, emotional stability, tact, and an outgoing personality are necessary in this profession. Physical therapy also takes a great deal of patience and the ability to work toward a long-range goal, even though the progress may sometimes seem slow. There are three education plans which prepare students for professional qualification in physical therapy. The first is a 4-year program leading to a bachelor's degree in physical therapy. The second is a 12- to 16-month certificate program for students who hold a bachelor's degree in a subject other than physical therapy. And last is a 2-year graduate program which leads to a master's degree for students with a bachelor's degree and the necessary background. Each of these plans includes a minimum of 4 months of clinical education and experience in health-care facilities where students care for patients under the supervision of a qualified physical therapist. The basic curriculum of an accredited program in physical therapy is generally divided into several areas: a liberal arts program which emphasizes the humanities and social studies; study of biological sciences including anatomy, physiology, and pathology; and a major emphasis in physical sciences like chemistry and physics, including the fundamental principles of mechanics, thermodynamics, light, sound, and electricity. Specialization courses provide the fundamental knowledge and skills required to treat patients, and supervised clinical practice is necessary to complete the course. Both the American Medical Association's Committee on Allied Health Education and Accreditation and the American Physical Therapy Association independently accredit educational programs in physical therapy.

All states, the District of Columbia, Virgin Islands, and Puerto Rico require licensure to practice physical therapy in the U.S. Each state, the District of Columbia, Virgin Islands and Puerto Rico have their own licensing requirements, and physical therapists must comply with the legal requirements of the area in which they practice.

Opportunities

Employment prospects for qualified physical therapists are expected to be favorable through the next decade. Many openings go unfilled each year because of the lack of physical therapists and the maldistribution of those who are available. In the near future, the greatest demand for physical therapists is expected in primary health care and preventive services, as well as in the traditional areas of rehabilitation.

Physical therapists can advance in several different ways. They may advance from staff physical therapist positions in hospital physical therapy departments to department director, and, if the service is large enough, they may advance to coordinator or director of rehabilitation services. Therapists who have a master's degree can advance to supervisory, administrative, or teaching positions.

XIII. PHYSICAL THERAPIST ASSISTANT
Physical Therapist Assistant
Physical Therapy Technician

Physical therapist assistants are skilled health practitioners who administer physical therapy to patients in treatment programs, under the direction of qualified physical therapists. They generally work with patients who have relatively stable conditions and use a variety of treatment techniques. They administer exercises; massage; heat, light, sound, water, electrical and infrared treatments; and use hot or cold packs to treat patients. Assistants instruct and assist patients to learn or improve their ability to walk, climb, and move from one location to another and to acquire skills needed for daily living. They observe patients during treatment to gather information on their responses and progress and report findings to the physical therapist, either orally or in writing. They also instruct patients in the use and care of artificial limbs, braces, and other devices such as crutches, canes, walkers, and wheelchairs.

Physical therapist assistants are employed in hospitals, rehabilitation centers, nursing homes, home-health agencies, public-health agencies, schools, private practices, and the armed forces.

Assistants work closely with patients, the patients' families, and other health-care personnel. They must be physically and mentally fit and be able to lift, climb, stoop, stand, and kneel. Additional requirements for physical therapist assistants are good hearing and visual acuity and the ability to communicate both orally and in writing.

Job Requirements

Preparation for this career area includes completion of high school and graduation from a 2-year accredited program leading to an associate degree in physical therapy. These programs are offered in junior and community colleges and combine academic studies with supervised clinical experience.

There are licensing requirements for physical therapist assistants in 23 states. The licensure boards in these states administer an examination to applicants who meet the qualification set forth in the State Physical Therapy Practice Act. At present, there are no certification requirements for physical therapist assistants. For information about licensing requirements, candidates should contact the appropriate state licensing agency.

Opportunities

The employment prospects for physical therapist assistant are good through the next several years. This outlook is based on the trend toward expanding physical therapy programs in many different types of facilities and on increased public awareness of the need for professional rehabilitation services.

Advancement in this work is based on work experience, which leads to greater responsibilities, and on advanced education. Assistants who engage in continued education can become fully qualified therapists by completing an accredited program of study.

XIV. PROSTHETIST

Prosthetists provide care to persons with partial or total loss of a limb by fitting and making artificial limbs known as prostheses. They consult with a physician, follow physician prescriptions, or help in developing prescriptions for the prostheses. Prosthetists talk with and examine patients and make recommendations for meeting their individual needs. After taking careful and accurate measurements and making any needed casts, they design the prosthesis, select the necessary materials, and prepare a layout of the design. Before completing the final model, they give the patient a fitting and make any necessary adjustments to insure that the device gives the patient comfort and function. Prosthetists instruct patients in the use and care of devices, maintain complete records of patient activity, and provide patients with the best possible care by keeping current on new technology in this field. Prosthetists supervise orthotic/prosthetic technicians and other laboratory workers engaged in making prostheses. Prosthetists engage in teaching activities or perform research work in this field. Some prosthetists are qualified, by additional training, to function as orthotists. In such cases, they carry the professional designation of prosthetist-orthotist.

Job Requirements

Persons considering this career are must have manual dexterity, be able to work with various types of tools, and possess mechanical ability. In addition, candidates must display patience, have a responsible attitude toward their work, and have a concern for detail and accuracy. Candidates must also have a sense of concern for the welfare of the disabled and be able to communicate effectively with both patients and members of the rehabilitation team. High school courses considered useful in preparing for this career include physics, chemistry, mathematics, biology, and shop courses in metal, wood, and plastics.

The American Board for Certification in Orthotics and Prosthetics is the certifying agency for professional practitioners in this field. They set education and training standards for prosthetists and administer an examination to all candidates applying for certification. The usual method of preparing for practitioner certification is to obtain a bachelor's degree in prosthetics from an accredited college or university, combined with 1 ear of clinical experience. However, persons who hold an associate degree in prosthetics or another area can also qualify by completing three specified courses in prosthetics at an accredited training facility and obtaining 2 years of clinical experience. Persons with a bachelor's degree in a different area of specialization may also qualify for practitioner certification by completing post-graduate training in prosthetics, ranging in length from 4 to 8 months, combined with 1 or 2 years of acceptable work experience. The minimum educational requirement will be a bachelor's degree.

Candidates who pass the certification examination are awarded the designation of Certified Prosthetist (CP). Those prosthetists who are also qualified to practice as orthotists, and who pass the examination in both specialties, are given the designation of Certified Prosthetist-Orthotist (CPO).

Opportunities

Employment prospects for qualified prosthetists are generally favorable and this trend is expected to continue during the next several years. Advancement in this field takes different forms, depending on the place of employment, but is generally based on work experience and level of skill. Qualified prosthetists often move into supervisory jobs, and in some cases may become self-employed as private practitioners.

XV. RECREATION THERAPIST
Activities Therapist
Recreation Specialist
Therapeutic Recreation Specialist

Recreation therapy is a specialized field in which recreation services are used to help individuals to recover from or adjust to illness, disability, or a specific social problem. Recreation therapists organize, develop, and carry out therapeutic recreational activities which help to meet this goal. These recreation programs are carried out in health facilities or community settings and include such activities as athletics, dancing, arts and crafts, music, movies, parties, gardening, and camping. Each of these is used to provide patients with the benefits of exercise, social participation, and group interaction. The therapeutic recreation activities that they conduct are designed to assist patients to develop interpersonal relationships, resocialize, relieve anxiety and tension, and develop confidence needed to participate in social activities.

Recreation therapists are an important part of the health team; they observe the physical, mental, and social progress of patients and contribute information and progress reports for use in meeting treatment goals. Recreation therapists assist patients in readjusting recreational needs to the activities offered by the community in which they live, based on knowledge of community resources and programs. Therapists also train groups of volunteers and students in techniques of recreation therapy. In addition, therapists work with various educational institutions to develop courses in the field of therapeutic recreation.

Recreation therapists are employed in a variety of public and private facilities including state or private hospitals for the mentally ill or mentally handicapped; prisons, and juvenile retention homes; orphanages; veterans' hospitals for both general and psychiatric patients; armed forces hospitals; homes for the aged; schools for the blind and rehabilitation centers for the physically handicapped. Others work in day-care centers, clinics, private and public schools, recreation centers, camp, and private community agencies. No general statement can be made about working conditions since they vary widely from facility to facility. Physical handicaps are not barriers to employment in this work as long as the individual has adjusted suitably to the disability.

Job Requirements

The educational minimum for entry as a professional in this field is a bachelor's degree in recreation, with emphasis on rehabilitation or therapeutic recreation, from an accredited college or university. In addition, students must complete 400 hours of clinical training in a university or college-affiliated hospital.

In some cases, an associate degree or certificate in therapeutic recreation is acceptable for entry into lower level jobs in this field, which involve limited responsibilities.

The American Association for Rehabilitation Therapy (AART) is the registration body for recreation therapists, and although registration is not a condition of employment, many therapists choose to do so. The requirements for registration as a recreation therapist include membership in AART, 2 years experience as a recreation therapist in a health-care facility, letters of recommendation, and copies of college transcripts.

Opportunities

Employment prospects for recreation therapists are favorable. The job market is expected to expand steadily in line with the expansion of health facilities throughout the country, as well as increases in population, particularly among the aging.

Advancement possibilities for recreation therapists vary widely among facilities, but, in general, promotions are based on experience, skill level, and education. In local, State, and Federal facilities, advancement can be achieved through the traditional methods of competitive civil service. Therapists in lower level positions who have an associate degree or certificate can advance to professional status in the field by completing the required bachelor's program in recreation. Therapists who obtain a master's degree can qualify for positions in administration, research, and teaching.

XVI. SPEECH PATHOLOGIST AND AUDIOLOGIST
Speech Correctionist
Speech and Language Pathologist/Audiologist
Speech Therapist

Speech pathologists and audiologists provide specialized help to people with problems of speaking and hearing. Speech-language pathologists are primarily concerned with persons who have speech language, and voice disorders, while audiologists concentrate on individuals with hearing problems.

The goal of speech pathologists and audiologists is to help children and adults overcome such problems as lisping, cleft palate, impaired hearing and talking difficulties resulting from cerebral palsy, emotional or physical disturbance or retardation, stuttering, or foreign dialect.

Speech pathologists diagnose and evaluate the individuals' speech and language abilities. They plan, direct, and conduct treatment programs to restore or develop patients' communication skills, regardless of the cause of the disorder. Speech pathologists can and do work closely with a number of other professionals, including audiologists, physicians, psychologists, social workers, counselors, physical and occupational therapists, and educators.

Audiologists are concerned with the prevention of hearing impairment and the conservation of hearing in children and adults. Audiologists assess the type and degree of hearing impairment. They then add their findings to educational, medical, social, behavioral, and other diagnostic data. After evaluating all of the available information, they may plan, direct, conduct, or participate in aural rehabilitation programs which meet the needs of the individual patient. These programs include such activities as hearing-aid selection and orientation, auditory training, speech reading, speech conservation, counseling, and guidance. Audiologists, like speech pathologists, often work closely with other professionals and as consultants to educational, medical, and other professional groups.

Speech pathologists and audiologists work in public and private schools; colleges and universities; clinics; research centers; hospitals; speech and hearing centers; private industry; private practice; and Federal, State, and local agencies.

Job Requirements

People who seek careers working directly with handicapped children and adults must have a real concern for people with physical and psychological problems and a sincere desire to help them. Equally important is the ability to work with such problems objectively. The potential speech pathologist or audiologist should have a warm, friendly personality that inspires confidence in the person being helped. Patience and perseverance are also needed, since rehabilitation may be a slow process. Relating well to children is a definite asset, since much of the work in speech rehabilitation is done with youngsters.

To qualify as a speech pathologist or audiologist, a person must have a master's degree in speech pathology or audiology. As part of the requirements for the master's degree, an individual will have numerous supervised clinical experiences. The student may also complete sufficient courses to be certified by the American Speech and Hearing Association (ASHA) and/or licensed by his or her state. A number of preprofessional degree programs in speech pathology or audiology are available.

Although programs leading to a master's degree in speech pathology or audiology vary from college to college, course work will include normal development and function of speech, language, and hearing; anatomy and physiology; the nature of disorders of speech, language, and hearing; the evaluation of speech, language, and hearing; clinical methods; and research.

Speech pathologists and audiologists may hold a variety of credentials, including State license, teaching credentials, and the American Speech and Hearing Association's Certificate of Clinical Competence in either or both areas. The ASHA certificates require academic training at the master's level, 1 year of experience in the field, and the passing of a national examination. Since credential and licensure requirements may vary from state to state, the appropriate state agency should be contacted to determine what requirements must be met.

Opportunities

Employment prospects are expected to increase. However, the competition for openings, especially in large urban areas, is expected to be keen.

Speech pathologists and audiologists may advance to administrative or supervisory positions such as clinic director or coordinator of clinical services. They may also become professors or department heads in colleges or universities, or choose to engage in research activities. Professional mobility is generally based on experience, skills, and level of education.

XVII. **VOCATIONAL REHABILITATION COUNSELOR**
Rehabilitation Counselor

Many different services go into rehabilitation—the process by which a sick or disabled person is restored to normal or near-normal functioning. One form of rehabilitation is concerned with repairing the damage done by illness or injury, and this is the responsibility of the physician. Another form of rehabilitation is concerned with restoring the person to a prior level of vocational performance or, if this is no longer possible, with preparing the individual for a new vocation. This is the function of vocational rehabilitation counseling. Most illnesses leave the patient with little or no residual handicap, while other may cause long-lasting or permanent damage to physical or mental functioning. Handicaps such as these may not only prevent the individual from taking up a former occupation, but may also demoralize the person to a point where the motivation to learn another trade or profession, or the courage to find another job, is no longer present.

Vocational rehabilitation counselors help handicapped or disabled persons to overcome these obstacles. Counselors help these persons decide on a realistic vocational goal and then help them work toward this goal—placement in a satisfactory job. This may involve not only extensive vocational training but also the reshaping of negative attitudes and the development of confidence and motivation. As soon as the injury or illness is brought under control and the patient is able to function again, vocational rehabilitation counselors help the individuals minimize any handicaps by capitalizing on other resources—aptitudes, skills, and interests. For example, counselors cannot create a new pair of eyes for a blinded watchmaker, but they can help by exploring other opportunities where manual deftness can be put to use, as in the production of electrical equipment. Through retraining, disabled workers learn to apply their abilities to new jobs, sometimes closely related, sometimes far removed from their previous work. Even in the case of handicapped or mentally handicapped young people who have never worked at all and who may have been considered unemployable, counselors can frequently devise a training program that can lead to employment.

To learn as much as possible about the handicapped person, counselors conduct interviews with the individual, the family doctor, former teachers, former employers, and others. Counselors may administer various aptitude tests and psychological tests or refer individuals to a testing specialist. If emotional problems seem to be interfering with adjustment, psychologists or psychiatrists may be consulted. When enough has been learned about the individual, the next step is to develop a vocational plan. Both individuals and counselors share in the planning, and others who may be involved are also called in—family members, prospective employers or social workers.

The actual training generally takes place in a sheltered job situation, where the trainee may learn a new occupation without the competitive pressures of regular employment. While training is in process, counselors keep in touch with trainees to observe progress and to be of continued help. When the training is completed, counselors help trainees to find jobs. Counselors make followup visits to insure that individuals are adjusting adequately to the new work situation. To be of greatest help, counselors must know the employment situation and employment opportunities, especially those for handicapped people. In cases where handicapped individuals are unable to enter or re-enter the labor market, counselors work with them to effect the best possible adjustment within family and social situations. In many cases, rehabilitation counselors specialize in services for particular groups—the blind, paraplegics, the mentally ill, and the mentally handicapped. In addition, counselors divide their time between counseling and community activities in the interest of the overall program—for example, calling on employers to solicit jobs, keeping in touch with educators and other interested professional groups, and taking part in meetings of local organizations and other activities which will help to focus public attention on problems of the handicapped and the benefits of rehabilitation.

Many vocational rehabilitation counselors work in state and local rehabilitation agencies which are financed by Federal and State funds. They also are employed by Veterans Administration facilities, rehabilitation centers, sheltered workshops, hospitals, labor unions, insurance companies, special schools, and public and private job-placement agencies. Counselors usually observe a typical 40-hour week, although they sometimes participate in various after-hours community activities related to rehabilitation, because of the importance of out-of-office contacts and community relations to vocational rehabilitation. In the course of the day's work, counselors are in touch with many people in many places—with the handicapped and their families, physicians and other members of the hospital staff, professional people in welfare agencies and similar organizations, school people, local public employment offices, employers' groups and individual employers, labor unions, and other sources of jobs or job information.

Job Requirements

The minimum requirement for a beginner's job in rehabilitation counseling is a bachelor's degree, preferably in psychology or education. However, employers are placing increasing emphasis on a master's degree in this area. Some experience in such related fields as vocational guidance and placement, personnel work, psychology, social work, or teaching also may be helpful. Master's programs require from 1½ to 2 years of study and include courses in rehabilitation problems, counseling techniques, vocational guidance, occupational and medical information, test administration and evaluation, psychology, statistics, and personnel administration. Additional courses may involve the community relations aspect of the rehabilitation program—for instance, public speaking, public relations, and methods of developing local job resources for the disabled. Some rehabilitation counselors take additional graduate work and earn a doctor's degree. This usually takes a total of from 4 to 6 years after college—part of it covered by the time required for the master's degree. Doctoral training usually goes into the more complex aspects of rehabilitation. This is supplemented by advanced work in the social sciences, and (as in other Ph.D programs) the student is expected to complete a considerable amount of original research.

There are currently no licensing requirements for vocational rehabilitation counselors, although licensing bills are beginning to be introduced in some states. However, some state agencies and private employers require some form of testing prior to offering employment, and increasingly they prefer individuals who are Certified Rehabilitation Counselors (CRCs). An individual is certified by the Commission on Rehabilitation Counselor Certification on the basis of an accepted level of competency, which includes both educational requirements and work experience. After receiving the initial certification, Certified Rehabilitation Counselors participate in a certification maintenance program to insure their continued proficiency in the field.

Opportunities

The present supply of rehabilitation counselors is inadequate to meet the needs of expanding groups of handicapped persons, and opportunities for qualified rehabilitation counselors are expected to remain good throughout the next decade. Counselors with graduate degrees in rehabilitation or a related field have the best opportunity for employment. Rehabilitation counselors can advance to supervisory or administrative positions after gaining sufficient experience and completing advanced training.

www.ingramcontent.com/pod-product-compliance
Lightning Source LLC
Chambersburg PA
CBHW081826300426
44116CB00014B/2496